SWEATERS
from the Maine Islands

SWEATERS
from the Maine Islands

■ *by* CHELLIE PINGREE *and* DEBBY ANDERSON ■
Photos by Peter Ralston

16 Knitting Patterns
from
NORTH ISLAND DESIGNS

YANKEE BOOKS

Camden, Maine

COVER AND TEXT DESIGN AND PRODUCTION: AMY FISCHER, CAMDEN, MAINE
Composition/Imagesetting: High Resolution, Camden, Maine
Printing: Metropole Litho, Quebec
Technical Knitting Editing: Dorothy T. Ratigan
Photography: Peter Ralston

Printed in Canada

Library of Congress Cataloging-in-Publication Data

Pingree, Chellie.
    Sweaters from the Maine islands : 16 knitting patterns from North Island Designs / by Chellie Pingree and Debby Anderson.
        p.   cm.
    Includes index.
    ISBN 0-89909-312-4
    1. Knitting—Maine—Patterns. 2. Sweaters—Maine. I. Anderson, Debby, 1940–
II. North Island Designs (Firm)   III. Title.
74813 US2M263   1990
746.8'2   dc20   90–12946
                                                                                  CIP

10 9 8 7 6 5 4 3 2 1

CONTENTS

WELCOME

Welcome to our third book combining knitting patterns with stories about a very small town. We are writing this book at the beginning of a new decade. Although no one can predict what that decade will bring, we are hoping that it will encompass those values that encourage knitting and the other elements of life that we advocate: participating in a community, whether it is

on your city block, at your place of work, or in a small rural town; caring about looking after your neighbor, by showing concern for our world environment or helping the single parent next door with her or his kids; and especially taking the time to live life to the fullest, to think, and to pursue those activities you enjoy. We think that knitting is ideal: it is a relaxing activity that allows you time for contemplation while you are making something wonderful.

For those of you who are unfamiliar with our company, we operate from an island twelve miles off the coast of Maine. The island has about four hundred year-round residents and the smallest kindergarten-through-twelfth-grade school in the state, with about sixty-five kids. This is a community where everyone knows everyone, and generally people don't lock their doors or take their keys out of their cars. Our small business of women ranging in age from their early twenties to over seventy puts together knitting kits and pattern books and tries to send a little of that island feeling to you.

This book features some of our favorite patterns, ones whose success as kits indicate that they are favorites with other knitters, too. We have included the lovely Lupine jacket—with our favorite wildflower embroidered on the sleeves. There is also Starry Night—the sweater that is perfect for men, women, and children. The design has wonderful simplicity and conveys the outline of our abundant spruce trees against a dark sky. It was inspired by the bright stars we see here every cloudless night.

The Windowbox—geraniums cascading from a windowbox of a clapboarded cottage—and the Loon sweater—dedicated to one of our favorite birds, whose piercing cry is known to anyone on the water—are included, as well as many more wonderful designs. We hope that you will enjoy knitting them and reading about the way of life that inspires us!

BEFORE YOU BEGIN KNITTING THESE PATTERNS . . .

For those of you who are knitting with our patterns for the first time, we've repeated Debby's knitting advice from our earlier books.

☐ GAUGE

Before you start any project—*check your gauge*. All sweaters are designed to be knit with a certain number of stitches to the inch, and this is far more important than the suggested needle size. Choose the needle size that will give you the required number of stitches to the inch.

To do this, knit a small swatch about 20 stitches wide by 3 inches high using the main color and the larger of the suggested needles. When you are done, gently press the swatch with a damp cloth, then let it cool. Now, measure 2 inches across and count the stitches; divide this number by two and you've got your gauge. If you have fewer stitches per inch than the gauge given in the pattern, decrease the size of your needles; if you have too many, increase the size of your needles and knit another swatch. No matter how many years you have been knitting, this step is crucial for achieving the results you want.

☐ RIBBING

When you are casting on the lower edge, remember that the ribbing is intended to be elastic when the garment is worn. If you have a tendency to cast on too tightly, use larger needles to cast on the stitches. Also remember to bind off neck stitches loosely so that the ribbing can stretch to go over the head.

When a pattern calls for K1, P1 ribbing, it is hard to go wrong. However, you will notice that in some of my patterns I have used a K2, P1 ribbing. When my sister-in-law was just

learning to knit, she very ambitiously started on one of our earlier designs. The next time she came to visit she proudly showed me the front, and I noticed she had done exactly what I said—K2, P1, but on both sides! It produced a unique look, to say the least, but it did not have the stretch of correctly knit ribbing. To avoid having her start over, I suggested she duplicate her ribbing on the back and cuffs. The lesson here is—work your ribbing K2, P1 on the right side and K1, P2 when you turn the piece over.

☐ NOTE

An edge stitch is worked in stockinette stitch on each edge of each piece for ease in assembly on all sweaters.

Before You Begin . . .

☐ Multicolor Knitting

Knitting with two or more colors is very easy, and if you have never done it before, now is a perfect time to start. Knit a small swatch to practice and you will be surprised how simple it is.

When knitting with two colors, don't tie a new color on until you have knit a few stitches with it—then go back and make a simple small knot. If you can weave the end in without making a knot at all, so much the better; but often if you don't attach it somehow, the stitches will have a tendency to loosen up. When you are carrying colors, it is important to carry the unused color for no more than 3 or 4 stitches before twisting the yarns together. If you carry it farther without twisting, you will end up with long strands on the inside that could catch when you put on the sweater.

It is good to use bobbins and short pieces of yarn and even attach new balls of the background color rather that carry the color behind. This way the design will lie flat and not pucker. You will be left with ends to weave in, but try to relax and enjoy it—a nice sweater takes time to complete.

Mistakes in two-color knitting can be corrected by working the correct color in duplicate stitch after the garment is complete. Duplicate stitch is also useful in areas where only a small amount of color is called for. A color out of place here or there won't make a great difference. As my mother used to say, "It will never be noticed on a galloping horse!"

☐ Putting Your Sweater Together

When all the pieces have been finished, be sure to press (block) them before sewing them together. To sew the seams, put the right sides together, take a straight needle (about a number 5) and use it as a large pin to hold the pieces while backstitching them together. Sew the shoulders first (unless the pattern has called for knitting them together), then the neck ribbing, the side seams, and the sleeve seams. Last of all, with the body wrong side out, insert the sleeve, right sides together, and match the seams at the underarms and shoulders. After the sleeve cap is fitted, backstitch it in place, and press all your seams.

Figuring out what size to make is a very logical process. Begin by finding a sweater that fits the way you (or your sweater recipient) would really like a sweater to fit. Then measure the chest, the sleeve length, the length of the sweater, etc. Here is where the stitch gauge becomes important again. If you want your sweater to measure 28 inches around the chest and there are 5 stitches per inch with the type of yarn you are using, you will need approximately 70 stitches each for the front and back, along with a couple of extra stitches for the seams. Check the pattern to see what size gives that number of stitches across the back.

EMBROIDERY

A few embroidery stitches can make a great addition to a sweater—a spark of color as well as texture, a way to make a garment unique. Here is an explanation of the simple stitches we included in some of the patterns in this book.

☐ **FRENCH KNOT**
This is the perfect stitch for little round things like apples or flowers in a field. Bring the yarn up through the sweater where you want the knot to be and wind the yarn around the needle 3 to 5 times, close to the sweater. Then insert the needle close by and, holding the twisted yarn with your thumb, pull the needle gently all the way through to form a knot.

☐ **OUTLINE STITCH**
This is somewhat like a backstitch except that each stitch starts just beside and behind the end of the previous stitch, creating a heavier line.

☐ **LOOP STITCH**
Bring the yarn up through the sweater to form a loop and insert the needle close to the same spot. Then bring the needle back up to catch the other end of the loop.

☐ **DUPLICATE STITCH**
Use this stitch to correct a mistake or to add a stitch in another color after the sweater is complete. Pull the needle up through the stitch below the one to be covered. Pass the needle under both sides of the stitch above the one to be covered and back down through the first stitch.

☐ **SATIN STITCHES**
Long and short stitch is a popular stitch for shading areas in a design. The stitch is worked very similar to the back stitch, but there is more color blending. Each stitch from the second row onward pierces the stitch right above it in the preceding row.

GLOSSARY OF TERMS	
approx	approximately
beg	beginning
CC	contrast color
dec	decrease, decreases
"	inch, inches
inc	increase, increases
K	knit
K2 tog	knit 2 together
MC	main color
oz	ounce
P	purl
PSSO	pass slipped stitch over
rem	remaining
rnd	round
st, sts	stitch, stitches
YO	yarn over

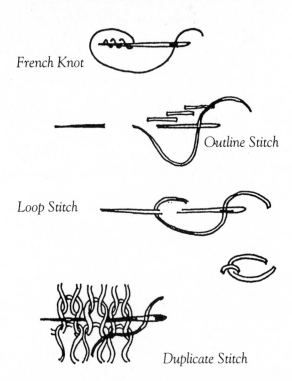

French Knot

Outline Stitch

Loop Stitch

Duplicate Stitch

EARLY MORNING

On our island work starts at 7 A.M. By 6:30 people are on their way to work, much of which centers around building and repairing houses and boats. Most of the men, and some of the women, are carpenters, painters, electricians, or plumbers; others work clearing trees, making cement, or moving dirt. These people deal with the essential components of our daily lives—shelter, electricity, water, heat, roads. Those who are not directly engaged in one of these areas provide supporting services for those who are, by doing clerical work, educating the community's children, or selling groceries. Everyone is involved in one way or another with the practical aspects of the island's life.

This makes our town different from the big cities of the world or other towns whose inhabitants earn their living manufacturing more esoteric things, such as computer chips,

potato chips, or school textbooks. How we make our money is evident in our conversations and in our skills. For instance, everyone knows a little bit about house construction. Many people build their own homes on the island. The entire family, including the children, participates in this process of building shelter, or at the very least observes. People often move into their homes before they are finished and complete the construction while living there, providing all the family members with a graphic illustration of how walls get finished, trim is added, and floors are laid. New house construction is something of a spectator sport in our community—homes under construction are often toured by the onlookers, who volunteer opinions and advice to the builders.

Dwellings may represent our basic

connection to the island, but as a community, we are involved with much more than shelter. Like consumers everywhere, we generate garbage. Every bag of trash that is created in our homes or businesses is one more bag that has to be hauled to the dump on the two days of the week it is open. On an island there's no ignoring this communal trash and what it does to our landscape and eventually to our groundwater.

Generally, people dress for the weather. Most people wear work clothes appropriate to their jobs, but even those who work at a desk usually don't follow high fashion. Not too many high heels—it may be muddy in the store parking lot, or there might be a big puddle at the gas pumps. Speaking of gas pumps—long before self-service gas was the trend on the mainland, it was the norm here. The owners of the only gas pumps in town are usually at work on a boat in their shop, and it seems silly to bother them. Most customers pump gas themselves (you have to master a vise-grip hanging on a broken lever to get the numbers back to zero) and bring in the cash. "Just right?" one of the owners will ask (no indoor digital meters here), and they always trust the customer to tell the truth.

Islanders talk about the weather and care about it because it affects their lives in a big way—woodstoves burn more wood, increasing the number of trips to the woodpile; the ferry doesn't run if it is too windy; and someone shingling outside in the winter will have less fun on an icy day than on a balmy one. Big storms bring down trees, sometimes causing us to lose power for extended periods, and they must be cleaned up.

This concern for fundamentals that unites our community is one of the things I treasure. When I think back to my suburban childhood where heat was controlled by a thermostat, garbage went into big trucks, and the weather rarely stopped anything, I realize how little I knew of the connection between my daily life and the earth. When people ask

me about the disadvantages of sending my kids to a sixty-five-pupil school, with an average of five to a graduating class, I explain that the education they receive in their daily lives goes a long way toward compensating for anything that may be lacking in our small school.

Because many of the issues that confront us as a nation and a planet pertain to our understanding of environmental processes, I think that any way of life that encourages us to become more aware of the source of our building materials, our role in creating and disposing of garbage, and the natural cycles on which all life depends constitutes an important education for all of us, young and old.

ADULT
VILLAGE SCENE PULLOVER

Sizes: 36 (38, 40)
Finished Sizes: 38 (40, 413/4)"
Needles:
    Size 5 and 8 or size needed to obtain stitch gauge of 41/2 sts = 1" using larger needles over stockinette stitch
    Size 5 16" circular needle
Materials:
    5 4 oz skeins Green Heather (MC) worsted weight yarn (1000 yds)
    1 4 oz skein Sky Blue worsted weight yarn (200 yds)
    50 yds White
    30 yds Light Green
    20 yds Dark Green
    20 yds Pink
    10 yds Light Brown
    10 yds Dark Brown
    10 yds Red
    10 yds Yellow

☐ NOTES

Any adjustment in body or sleeve length should be made before beginning second cable grouping prior to armhole shaping.

☐ PATTERN STITCHES

C6B – Cable 6 Back – place 3 sts on holder to back of work, K3, K3 from holder.
C6F – Cable 6 Front – place 3 sts on holder to front of work, K3, K3 from holder.

☐ FRONT

With smaller needles and MC, cast on 74 (80, 86) sts.
Row 1: K2, *P1, K2, rep from * to end.
Row 2: Knit the knits and purl the purls. Rep these 2 rows for 31/4", inc 12 (10, 8) sts on last row of rib — 86 (90, 94) sts. Change to larger needles and work as follows:
Row 1: K14 (16, 18), (P2, K6) twice, P2, K22, (P2, K6) twice, P2, K14 (16, 18).
Row 2 and all even-numbered rows: Knit the knits and purl the purls.
Rows 3, 5, 9, 11 and 13: Same as Row 1.
Rows 7 and 15: K14 (16, 18), (P2, C6B)

twice, P2, K22, (P2, C6F) twice, P2, K14 (16, 18). Rep Rows 1 and 2 until work measures 111/2 (12, 12)" from beginning or 21/2" less than desired length to underarm, ending with a wrong-side row. Right side facing, work Rows 7 – 16, then Row 1. Wrong side facing, knit 3 rows forming 2 ridges on right side of work. Length to underarm is 14 (141/2, 141/2)". **Begin body chart.** *Armhole shaping:* At beg of next 2 rows, bind off 5 sts. Dec 1 st at each end of needle every other row 5 times — 66 (70, 74) sts. Continue with chart to neck opening. Right side facing, work 23 (25, 27) sts, place center 20 sts on holder, join new ball of yarn, work to end. Purl back. Working both sides at the same time, at each neck edge dec 1 st every other row 4 times — 19 (21, 23) sts. Work to end of chart binding off shoulder sts as per chart.

☐ BACK

Work patterns as for Front including armhole shaping. Follow charted design straight to shoulders, binding off shoulder sts as per chart. Place center 28 sts on holder.

☐ SLEEVES

With smaller needles and MC, cast on 44 (44, 50) sts.
Row 1: K2, *P1, K2, rep from * to end.
Row 2: Knit the knits and purl the purls. Rep these 2 rows for 3", inc 0 (4, 0) sts on last row of rib — 44 (48, 50) sts. Change to larger needles and work as follows:
Row 1: K13 (15, 16), (P2, K6) twice, P2, K13, (15, 16). Work cable pattern same as Front while inc 1 st each end of needle every 8th row 9 times — 62 (66, 68) sts. Work until sleeve measures 141/2" from beginning or 21/2" less than desired length to underarm, ending with a wrong-side row. Right side facing, work Rows 7 – 16, then Row 1. Wrong side facing, knit 3 rows forming 2 ridges on right side of work. Length to underarm is 17". **Begin sleeve chart.** *Sleeve cap:* At beg of next 2 rows, bind off 5 sts. Dec

1 st each end of needle every other row until 20 sts remain. At beg of next 4 rows, bind off 3 sts. Bind off rem 8 sts.

☐ FINISHING

Sew shoulder seams. Using smaller circular needle, pick up 75 sts around neck, including sts on holders, and work K2, P1 rib for 1". Bind off loosely with larger needle. Set in sleeves, sew remaining seams, weave in all ends.

Sky = blue
⊡ = light green
⊞ = dark green
⊙ = white
■ = dark brown
◣ = red
⊠ = purl instead of knit or vice versa

Chart for Sleeve

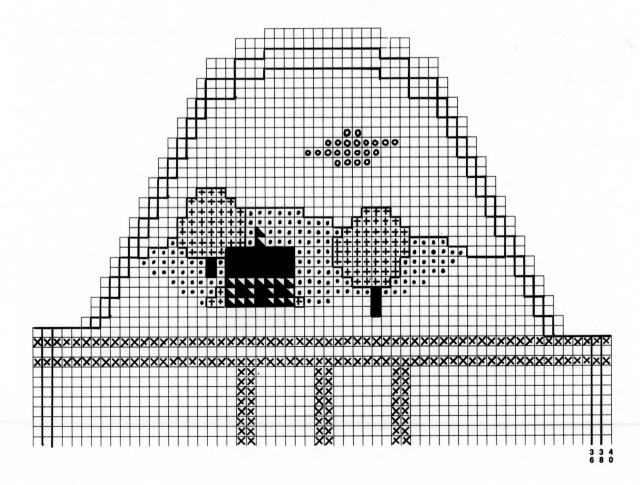

3 3 4
6 8 0

Adult Village Scene Pullover

Child's Village Scene Pullover

CHILD'S
VILLAGE SCENE PULLOVER

Sizes: 6 (8, 10, 12)
Finished Sizes: 25 (27, 28, 30)"
Needles:
  Size 4 and 7 or size needed to obtain stitch gauge of 5 sts = 1" using larger needles over stockinette stitch
  Size 4 16" circular needle
Materials:
  3 (3, 4, 4) 4 oz skeins Green Heather (MC) worsted weight yarn (600 – 800 yds)
  1 4 oz skein Sky Blue worsted weight yarn (200 yds)
  100 yds White
  30 yds Light Green
  20 yds Dark Green
  20 yds Pink
  10 yds Light Brown
  10 yds Dark Brown

☐ NOTES
Any adjustment in body or sleeve length should be made before beginning second cable grouping prior to armhole shaping.

☐ PATTERN STITCHES
C4B – Cable 4 Back – place 2 sts on holder to back of work, K2, K2 from holder.
C4F – Cable 4 Front – place 2 sts on holder to front of work, K2, K2 from holder.

☐ FRONT
With smaller needles and MC, cast on 62 (68, 68, 74) sts.
Row 1: K2, *P1, K2, rep from * to end.
Row 2: Knit the knits and purl the purls. Rep these 2 rows for 21/2", inc 2 (0, 2, 2) sts on last row of rib — 64 (68, 70, 76) sts. Change to larger needles and work as follows:
Row 1: K7 (9, 10, 13), (P2, K4) twice, P2, K22, (P2, K4) twice, P2, K7 (9, 10, 13).
Row 2 and all even-numbered rows: Knit the knits and purl the purls.
Rows 3, 7 and 9: Same as Row 1.
Rows 5 and 11: K7 (9, 10, 13), (P2, C4B) twice, P2, K22, (P2, C4F) twice, P2, K7 (9, 10, 13). Rep Rows 1 and 2 until work

measures 8 (9, 91/2, 10)" from beginning or 2" less than desired length to underarm, ending with a wrong-side row. Right side facing, work Rows 5 – 12, then Row 1. Wrong side facing, knit 3 rows forming 2 ridges on right side of work. Length to underarm is 10 (11, 111/2, 12)". **Begin body chart.** *Armhole shaping:* At beg of next 2 rows, bind off 2 (3, 3, 5) sts. Dec 1 st at each end of needle every other row 3 (3, 4, 4) times — 54 (56, 56, 58) sts. Continue with chart to neck opening. Right side facing, work 19 (20, 20, 21) sts, place center 16 sts on holder, join new ball of yarn, work to end. Purl back. Working both sides at the same time, at each neck edge dec 1 st every other row twice — 17 (18, 18, 19) sts. Work to end of chart binding off shoulder sts as per chart.

☐ BACK
Work patterns as for Front including armhole shaping. Follow charted design straight to shoulders, binding off shoulder sts as per chart. Place center 20 sts on holder.

☐ SLEEVES
With smaller needles and MC, cast on 32 (32, 38, 38) sts.
Row 1: K2, *P1, K2, rep from * to end.
Row 2: Knit the knits and purl the purls. Rep these 2 rows for 21/2 (21/2, 21/2, 3)", inc 4 (6, 2, 4) sts on last row of rib — 36 (38, 40, 42) sts. Change to larger needles and work as follows:
Row 1: K11 (12, 13, 14), (P2, K4) twice, P2, K11 (12, 13, 14). Work cable pattern same as Front while inc 1 st each end of needle every 6th row 6 times — 48 (50, 54, 58) sts. Work until sleeve measures 10 (11, 12, 13)" from beginning or 2" less than desired length to underarm, ending with a wrong-side row. Right side facing, work Rows 5 – 12, then Row 1. Wrong side facing, knit 3 rows forming 2 ridges on right side of work. Length to underarm is 12 (13, 14, 15)". **Begin sleeve chart.** *Sleeve cap:* At beg of next 2 rows, bind

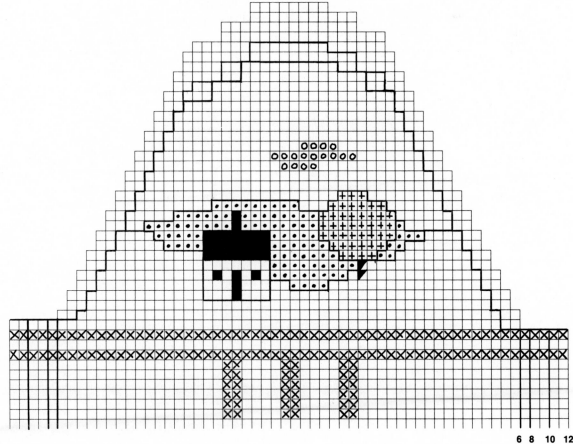
off 2 (3, 3, 5) sts. Dec 1 st each end of needle every other row until 22 (20, 20, 20) sts remain. At beg of next 4 rows, bind off 3 sts. Bind off rem 10 (8, 8, 8) sts.

☐ FINISHING

Sew shoulder seams. Using smaller circular needle, pick up 75 sts around neck, including sts on holders, and work K2, P1 rib for 1". Bind off loosely with larger needle. Set in sleeves, sew remaining seams, weave in all ends.

Sky = blue
▫ = **light green**
⊞ = **dark green**
■ = **brown**
◤ = **light brown**
⊙ = **white**
⊠ = **purl instead of knit or vice versa**

On one sleeve have a yellow house. On the other sleeve, a red house.

Chart for Sleeve

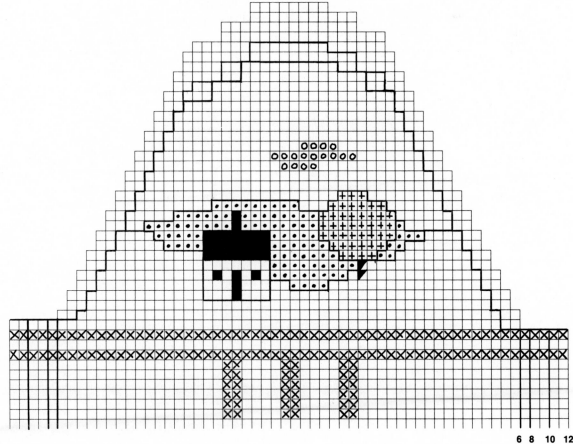

6 8 10 12

ADULT VILLAGE SCENE PULLOVER

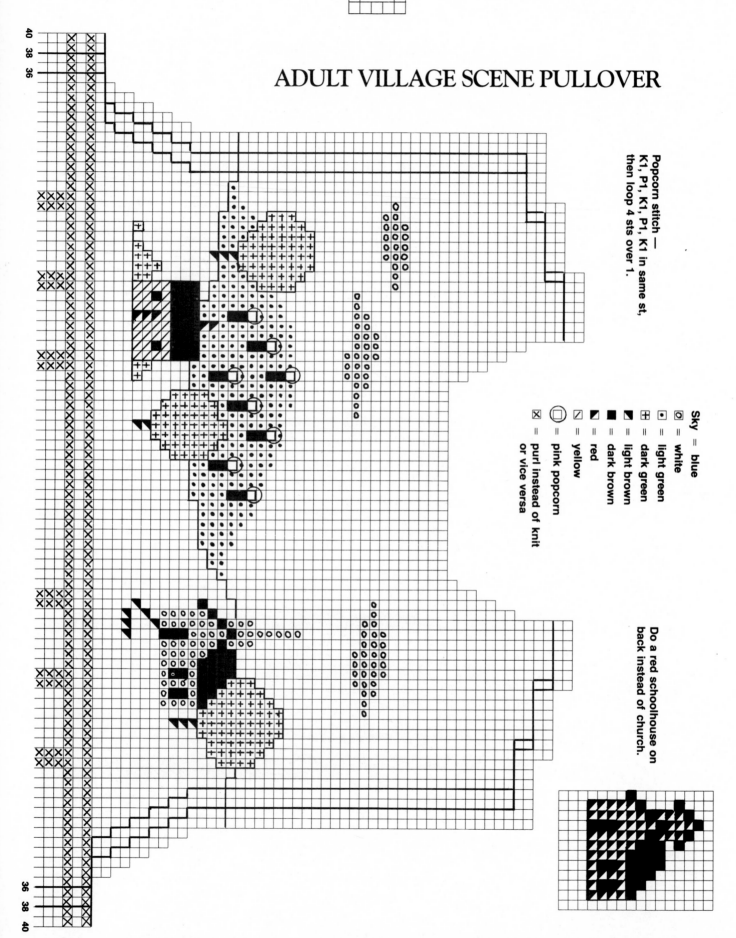

Popcorn stitch —
K1, P1, K1, P1, K1 in same st,
then loop 4 sts over 1.

Sky = blue
⊡ = white
• = light green
✢ = dark green
◻ = light brown
◼ = dark brown
◪ = red
◻ = yellow
◯ = pink popcorn
☒ = purl instead of knit
     or vice versa

Do a red schoolhouse on
back instead of church.

CHILD'S VILLAGE SCENE PULLOVER

Popcorn stitch —
K1, P1, K1, P1, K1 in same st,
then loop 4 sts over 1.

Sky = Blue

◯ = pink popcorn

⊙ = white
◣ = light brown
■ = dark brown
• = light green
✛ = dark green
☒ = purl instead of knit
or vice versa

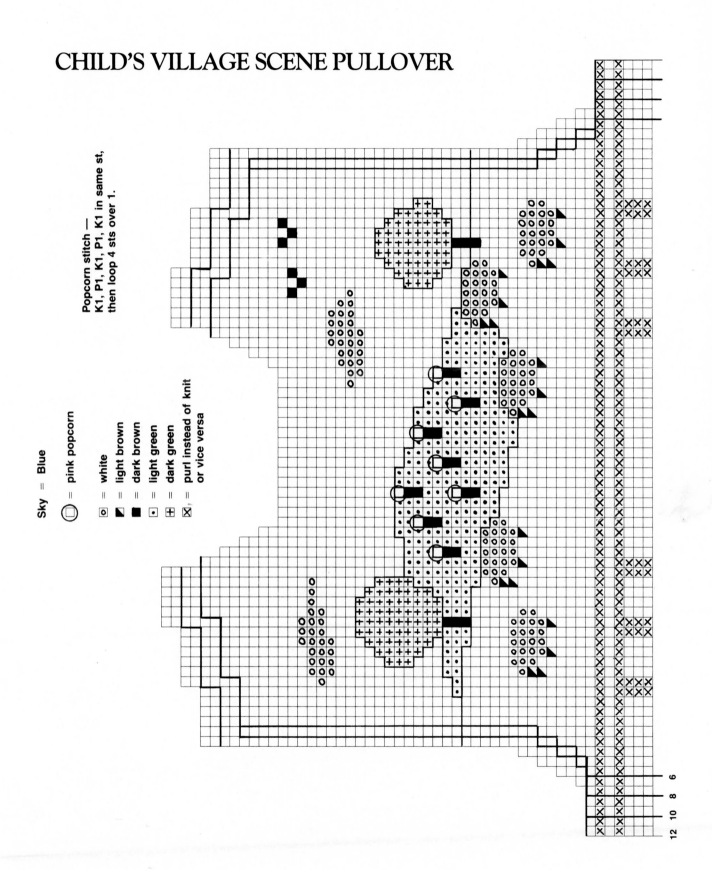

12 10 8 6

Lupine Jacket

THE LUPINE

Wildflowers bloom in our woods and fields when the weather turns warm. The first flowers to appear are the wood violets, and the last, blooming well into the fall, are the goldenrod. The most spectacular displays are in June and early July, with daisies, Indian paintbrush, and most notably lupines. Appearing like cultivated flowers that have escaped their boundaries, these large, spreading flowers are abundant in poor gravelly soils, favoring fields, hillsides, and occasionally roadsides.

The wild lupine, *Lupinus perennis*, is usually one to two feet high, with tall spiked flowers. The majority of the blossoms are blue or purple, but pink, magenta, and white are sprinkled among the stands. Lupines have beautiful palmlike leaves that are divided into seven leaflets.

Although they can be seen along the road, individually or in groups of two or three plants, lupines will also cover large fields or hillsides with color. We all have our favorite viewing spots and colors to watch for. People will often remark about a particularly brilliant magenta or pink lupine that they spied in a field. Occasionally you will notice a stalk with a string or band of cloth tied to it—the only way to remember which stalk had the perfect color when you want to go back to retrieve the seeds.

Lupines do not transplant well because they have very deep taproots that tend to break when the plants are being dug up. (The taproot explains how lupines survive in dry areas—the plant is able to search deep for its water.) However, they are easy to grow from the seeds that become available later in the summer, after the flowers have matured. When I first came to the community, my job was helping in the garden of a summer person who had retired here to live year-round. She and her husband had fixed up an old house and landscaped the area around it, which was once a gravel pit. Over the years she had transformed the "pit" behind her house into a colorful slope of lupines. She had me gather the seed pods and continue to spread them around, in order to encourage the lupines to move even farther up the bank.

Some people think that the name *lupine* comes from the Greek *lupe*, which means grief, because the seeds are extremely bitter when eaten raw. The more common derivation is traced to the Latin *lupus*, meaning wolf, because it was thought that these plants devoured the fertility of the soil. Although this notion was probably the conventional wisdom at one time, we now know that, as members of the pea family, these plants are capable of fixing air-borne nitrogen on their roots and leaving it in the soil when they die. This means that lupines play an important part in increasing the fertility of marginal soils. In some places farmers actually plant them as cover crops.

On the island, lupines are a sure sign of summer's arrival and a cue to pay attention to the few hot days and balmy nights that will pass by all too quickly. They are also a reminder of the amazing beauty that drifts in and out of our lives through no effort of our own.

LUPINE FITTED JACKET

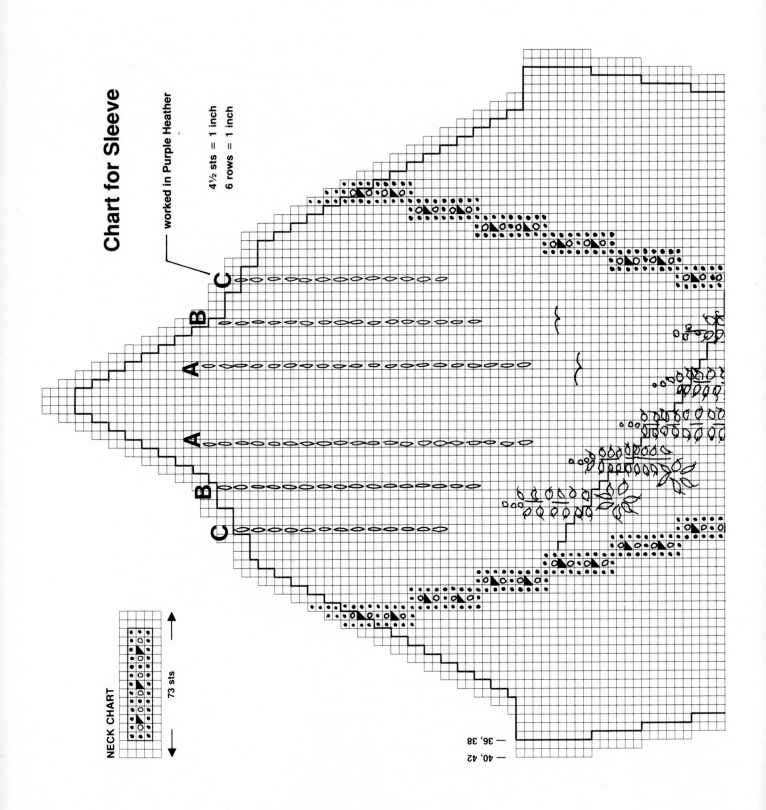

Chart for Sleeve

worked in Purple Heather

4½ sts = 1 inch
6 rows = 1 inch

C
B
A
A
B
C

NECK CHART

73 sts

— 36, 38
— 40, 42

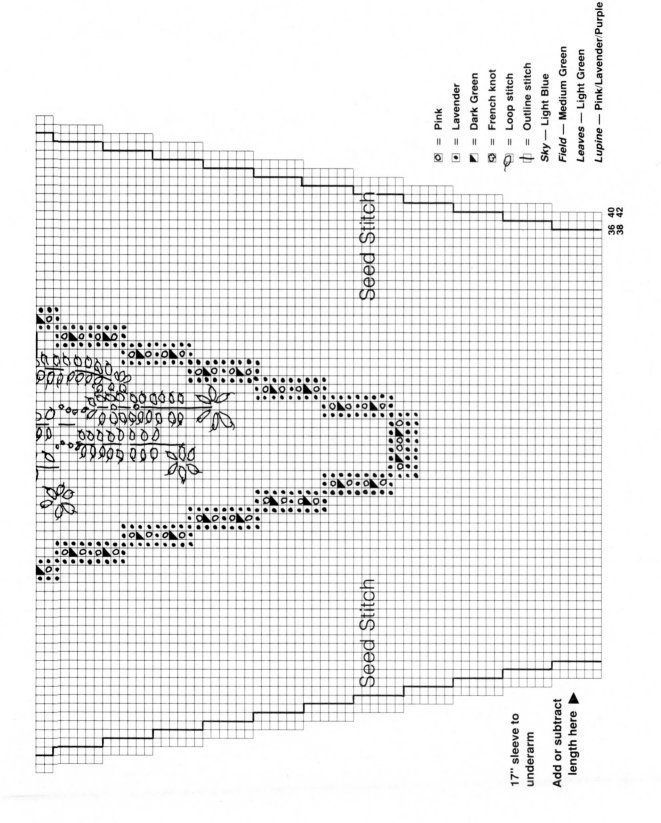

Seed Stitch

Seed Stitch

⊙ = Pink
⊡ = Lavender
◣ = Dark Green
❀ = French knot
⟋ = Loop stitch
⌓ = Outline stitch

Sky — Light Blue

Field — Medium Green

Leaves — Light Green

Lupine — Pink/Lavender/Purple

36 40
38 42

17" sleeve to
underarm

Add or subtract
length here ▲

LUPINE AND PRUSSIAN FITTED JACKETS

This sweater is designed to be short and fitted. Chest measurement is the same as the finished size. Length to underarm is 91/2 (10, 10, 101/2)".

Sizes: 36 (38, 40, 42)
Finished Sizes: 36 (38, 40, 42)"
Needles:
   Size 5 and 7 or size needed to obtain stitch gauge of 5 sts and 7 rows = 1" using smaller needles over stockinette stitch
   41/2 sts and 6 rows = 1" using larger needles over seed stitch
   Size D/3 crochet hook
Materials for Lupine Jacket:
   5 4 oz skeins Deep Blue Heather (mc) worsted weight yarn (1000 yds)
   1 4 oz skein Light Blue Heather worsted weight yarn (200 yds)
   100 yds Medium Green Heather worsted weight yarn
   75 yds Purple Heather worsted weight yarn
   25 yds Dark Green worsted weight yarn
   75 yds Forest Green fingering weight yarn for trim
   50 yds Pink fingering weight yarn
   25 yds Deep Purple fingering weight yarn
   25 yds Light Green fingering weight yarn
   9 pewter buttons

Materials for Prussian Jacket:
   5 4 oz skeins Wine (MC) worsted weight yarn (1000 yds)
   11/2 4 oz skeins Navy worsted weight yarn (300 yds)
   100 yds White worsted weight yarn
   50 yds Pink Heather worsted weight yarn
   75 yds Navy fingering weight yarn for trim
   9 pewter buttons

□ NOTES
1. Body is knit on smaller needles. Sleeves are knit on larger needles. Sleeve extension on chart is a small shoulder pad and stitched to inside of shoulder seam.
2. Work embroidery for Lupine Jacket using triple strand fingering yarn.
3. Long stripes are worked in Purple Heather for Lupine, Pink for Prussian.
4. Knitted pattern on sleeves is worked in stockinette stitch.

□ PATTERN STITCH
Seed Stitch
Row 1: *K1, P1, rep from * over designated sts.
Row 2: Knit the purls and purl the knits.

□ RIGHT FRONT
With smaller needles and MC, cast on 43 (42, 45, 47) sts. Following chart for your size, keep side panel in K1, P1 ribbing for 18 rows, then work seed st above ribbing. Front panel is worked in stockinette st. Work buttonholes as follows: Purl across row to last 5 sts. Bind off 2 sts, P3 sts. *Next row:* K3, cast on 2 sts firmly above bound-off sts, finish row. *Armhole shaping:* Following chart, bind off 5 (8, 8, 10) sts. Dec 1 st same edge every other row 5 (5, 6, 6) times. Continue in patterns as established and inc 1 st at armhole edge every 4 rows 4 (4, 2, 2) times **and at the same time**, work Neck shaping: Bind off 4 sts, K9, place these 9 sts on holder, finish row. Dec 1 st at neck edge every other row 5 times. Bind off shoulders as indicated on chart.

□ LEFT FRONT
Work same as Right Front, reversing shaping and omitting buttonholes.

□ BACK
Using smaller needles and MC, cast on 88 (94, 100, 104) sts. Keeping center 42 sts in stockinette st, work side panels to match Fronts. Follow chart to shoulders. Bind off shoulders same as Fronts. Place 28 back neck sts on holder.

☐ **SLEEVES**

Using smaller needles and MC, cast on 40 (40, 42, 42) sts. Work 22 rows of K1, P1 ribbing. Inc 10 (10, 12, 12) sts evenly across last row of ribbing. Change to larger needles and work in seed st. Follow chart, inc 1 st each end of needle every 6th row 14 times. To work long vertical stripes, attach yarn on wrong side row, P1; on right side, slip the stitch.

When sleeves are completed, block. Press pleats at top of sleeve by folding point A over onto point C. Attach at upper edge. On inside, attach both B points together at center.

☐ **FINISHING**

Sew shoulder seams. With smaller needles and MC, pick up and knit 9 sts from right front neck, 14 sts at right neck edge, 28 sts from back neck, 13 sts at left neck edge, and 9 sts from left front neck — 73 sts. **Work chart for neck.** This chart is abbreviated to show beginning and end. Repeat motif across neck.

Right sides tog and using backstitch, sew side seams and sleeve seams. Turn body wrong side out and insert sleeve cap in armhole, right sides tog, edges even, matching underarm and shoulders, sew seam using backstitch, disregarding tab which will serve as shoulder pad. Attach end of tab to shoulder seam.

Crochet edge: With crochet hook and specified yarn and wrong side facing, start on lower edge of middle panel of back. Work 2 single crochet sts in every other available st along lower back, up edge of stockinette st panel, along shoulder edge, down edge of left front stockinette st panel, along lower edge of left front, up front edge, around neck, all around right front back, over right shoulder, and down back to beginning.

Sew on buttons, weave in ends, press seams, and block entire sweater.

LUPINE AND PRUSSIAN FITTED JACKET

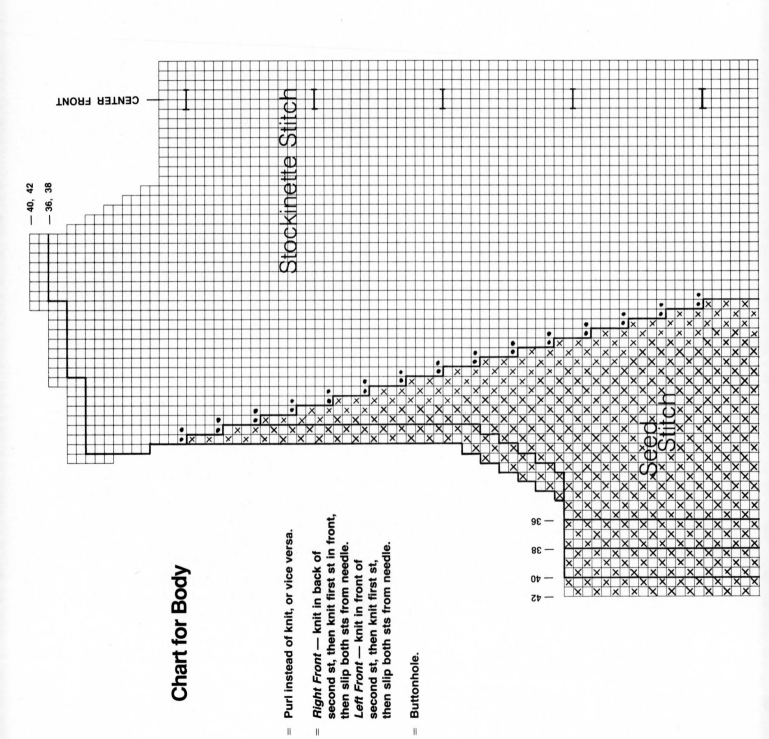

Chart for Body

CENTER FRONT

Stockinette Stitch

Seed Stitch

— 40, 42
— 36, 38

⊠ = Purl instead of knit, or vice versa.

⊡/⊡ = *Right Front* — knit in back of second st, then knit first st in front, then slip both sts from needle.
Left Front — knit in front of second st, then knit first st, then slip both sts from needle.

I = Buttonhole.

36
38
40
42

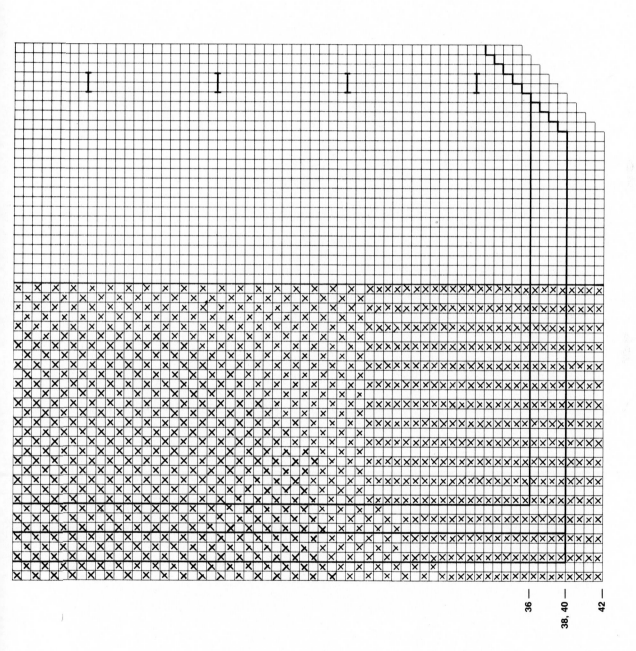

36 —

38, 40 —

42 —

This sweater is designed to be a short, fitted jacket. Finished length to underarm is approx 11 in for a size 38. Please check your measurements and decide on length before you begin.

Holly Jacket

Prussian Jacket

PRUSSIAN FITTED JACKET

NECK CHART

73 sts

4½ sts = 1 inch
6 rows = 1 inch

Chart for Sleeve

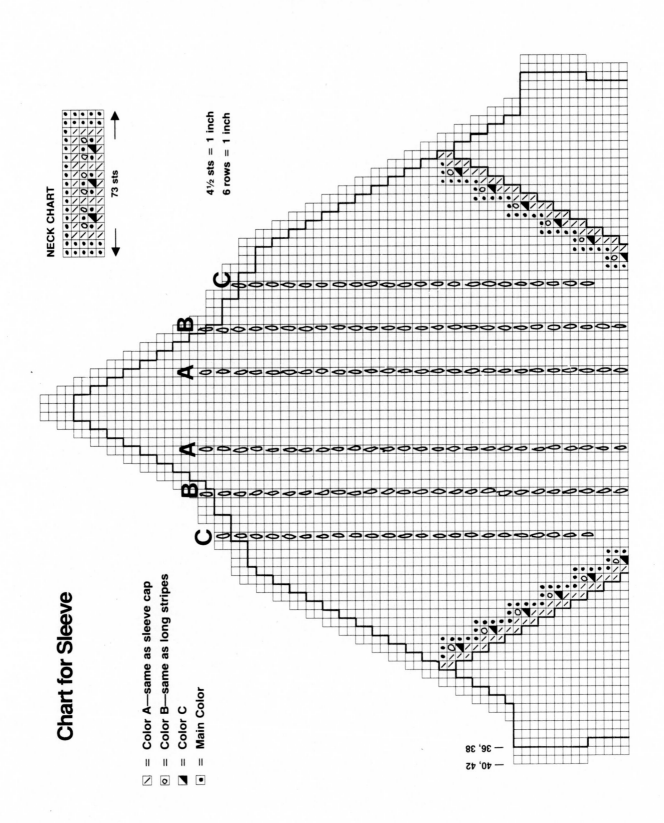

☑ = Color A—same as sleeve cap

◯ = Color B—same as long stripes

◣ = Color C

• = Main Color

—40, 42
—36, 38

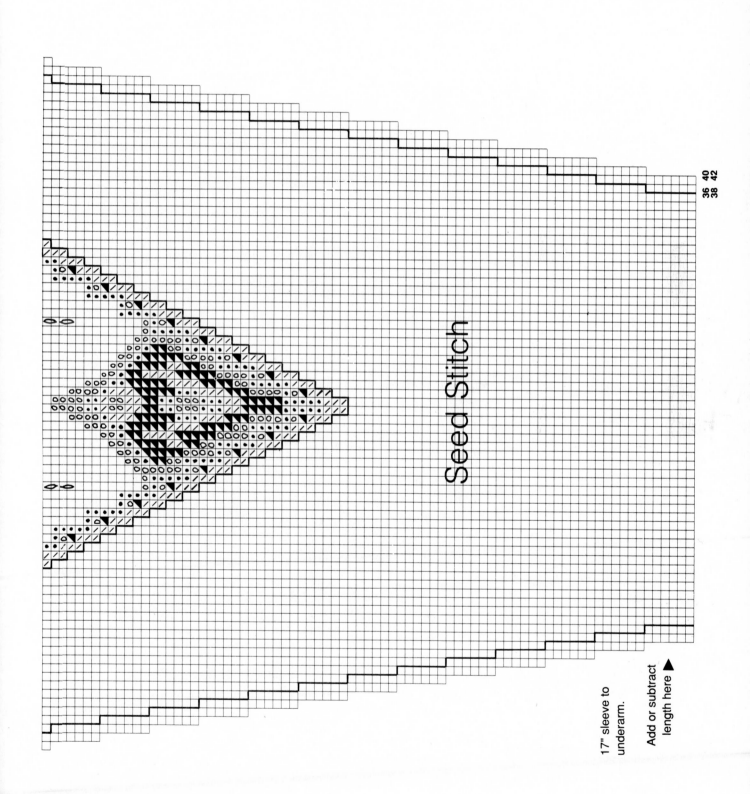

Seed Stitch

36 40
38 42

17" sleeve to
underarm.

Add or subtract
length here ▲

HOLLY
FITTED JACKET

As with the Lupine and Prussian Jackets, this sweater is designed to be short and fitted. Chest measurement is the same as the finished size. Length to underarm is 91/2 (10, 10, 101/2)".

Sizes: 36 (38, 40, 42)
Finished Sizes: 36 (38, 40, 42)"
Needles:
    Size 5 and 7 or size needed to obtain stitch gauge of 5 sts and 7 rows = 1" using smaller needles over stockinette stitch
    41/2 sts and 6 rows = 1" using larger needles over seed stitch
    Size 3 double pointed needles (dpn)
Materials:
    6 4 oz skeins Cranberry (MC) worsted weight yarn (1200 yds)
    50 yds Dark Green worsted weight yarn
    125 yds Dark Green fingering yarn for trim
    9 pewter buttons
    5 yds red yarn for berries
    For Chickadee: small amounts crewel yarn in White, Tan, Gray and Black
    Small square muslin and iron-on interfacing

☐ NOTES
1. Body is knit on smaller needles. Sleeves are knit on larger needles. Sleeve extension on chart is a small shoulder pad and stitched to inside of shoulder seam.
2. Work trim using double strand fingering yarn.

☐ PATTERN STITCHES
Seed Stitch
Row 1: *K1, P1, rep from * over designated sts.
Row 2: Knit the purls and purl the knits.

Mock Cable
Row 1: Skip first st, K second st on needle, then K first st.
Rows 2 and 4: P2
Row 3: K2.

☐ RIGHT FRONT
With smaller needles and MC, cast on 43 (42, 45, 47) sts. Following chart for your size, keep side panel in K1, P1 ribbing for 18 rows, then work seed st above ribbing. Front panel is worked in stockinette st. Work buttonholes as follows: Purl across row to last 5 sts. Bind off 2 sts, P3 sts. *Next row:* K3, cast on 2 sts firmly above bound-off sts, finish row. *Armhole shaping:* Following chart, bind off 5 (8, 8, 10) sts. Dec 1 st at same edge every other row 5 (5, 6, 6) times. Continue in patterns as established and inc 1 st at armhole edge every 4 rows 4 (4, 2, 2) times ***and at the same time*** work Neck shaping: Bind off 4 sts, K9, place these 9 sts on holder, finish row. Dec 1 st at neck edge every other row 5 times. Bind off shoulders as indicated on chart.

☐ LEFT FRONT
Work same as Right Front, reversing shaping and omitting buttonholes.

☐ BACK
With smaller needles and MC, cast on 88 (94, 100, 104) sts. Keeping center 42 sts in stockinette st, work side panels to match Fronts. Follow chart to shoulders. Bind off shoulders same as Fronts. Place 28 back neck sts on holder.

☐ SLEEVES
With smaller needles and MC, cast on 40 (40, 42, 42) sts. Work 22 rows of K1, P1 ribbing. Inc 10 (10, 12, 12) sts evenly across last row of ribbing. Change to larger needles and work in seed st. On Row 33, with MC, work in seed st to center 6 sts, attach CC and work 6 sts in stockinette st, continue with MC in seed st to end of row. On row 35, work in seed st to center 6 sts, K2 CC, K2 MC, attach second ball of CC and K2, continue with MC in seed st to end of row. On 37th row, work over to 1 st before CC. Slip 1 MC st and 2 CC sts to dpn. Turn dpn to the right so the CC sts are at right edge of needle. K2

CC, P1 MC, Mock Cable in MC, slip 2 CC sts and 1 MC st to dpn. Turn dpn around to the left, P1 MC, K2 CC, work to the end of row. Repeat this process on every 4th row as per chart. It creates a nice twisted cable in the CC as it incorporates the MC sts into the center panel.

LEAVES

Holly Leaves (6 large, 2 small) are knit separately, then sewn in place. Holly berries are French knots worked in red.

With size 3 dpn and Green fingering yarn (doubled), cast on 3 sts.

Row 1: K1, K in front, back, front of next st (FBF), K1.

Row 2: P5

Row 3: K2, knit FBF, K2.

Row 4: P7.

Row 5: Bind off 2, knit FBF, K1, turn.

Row 6: Bring yarn to front of work, reach over and pass 1 st over the other on left needle, slip 1 st to right needle, pass 1 st over the other, bring yarn to back, P4.

Repeat rows 3-6 once.

Repeat rows 3-4 once.

Next Row: Bind off 3, K1, turn.

Last row: Bring yarn to front of work, reach over and pass 1 st over the other on left needle, slip 1 st to right needle, pass 1 st over the other, P1, bind off 1, break yarn and slip through remaining st.

For a smaller holly leaf, work rows 1-6, repeat rows 3-4, then work last 2 rows.

FINISHING

Sew side and sleeve seams. Set in sleeves, stitching down shoulder pad. Sew on buttons. Sew on holly leaves. Embroider French knots.

TRIM

Instead of crocheting an edge, I used an "idiot cord." With size 3 dpn and Green fingering yarn (doubled), cast on 3 sts. Starting with right side of sweater facing you, at the lower left-hand corner of back panel, where stockinette sts meet ribbing, pick up and K1

st. Pass last st of cast-on sts over it. Pick up one more st. Slide sts to right-hand end of needle. K2, slip 1 as if to purl, K1 in back, PSSO, pick up one more st, slide sts to other end and repeat. It sounds confusing but creates a very nice corded edge. Work about every 3 out of 4 sts. When doing a corner, knit an extra row either side of corner st to get a nice square corner. Work every available st around neck, otherwise neck becomes too tight. I worked a second cord along bottom edge of right front, up front, around neck, down other front, and along bottom edge of left front.

CHICKADEE

Use steam iron with metal sole plate. Place square of interfacing shiny side down over chickadee. Trace outline using a soft lead pencil. Set iron at medium/steam. Iron interfacing onto muslin. Press firmly down for 10 full seconds. DO NOT SLIDE IRON. Let fabric cool before checking bond. Work crewel sts (satin and backstitch) in designated colors. When finished, clip muslin 1/4" around chickadee. Turn to inside and hand hem. Stitch to jacket following photograph.

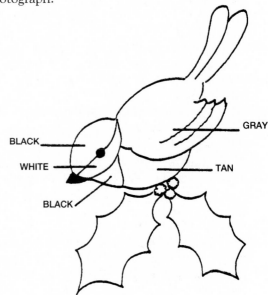

BLACK

WHITE

BLACK

GRAY

TAN

HOLLY FITTED JACKET

Chart for Sleeve

4½ sts = 1 inch
6 rows = 1 inch

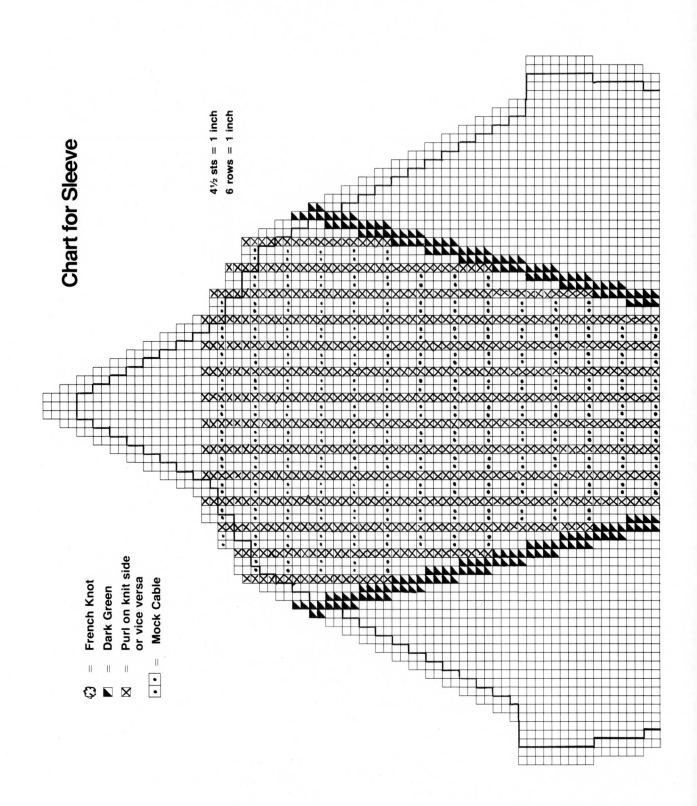

❀ = French Knot

◣ = Dark Green

☒ = Purl on knit side or vice versa

• = Mock Cable

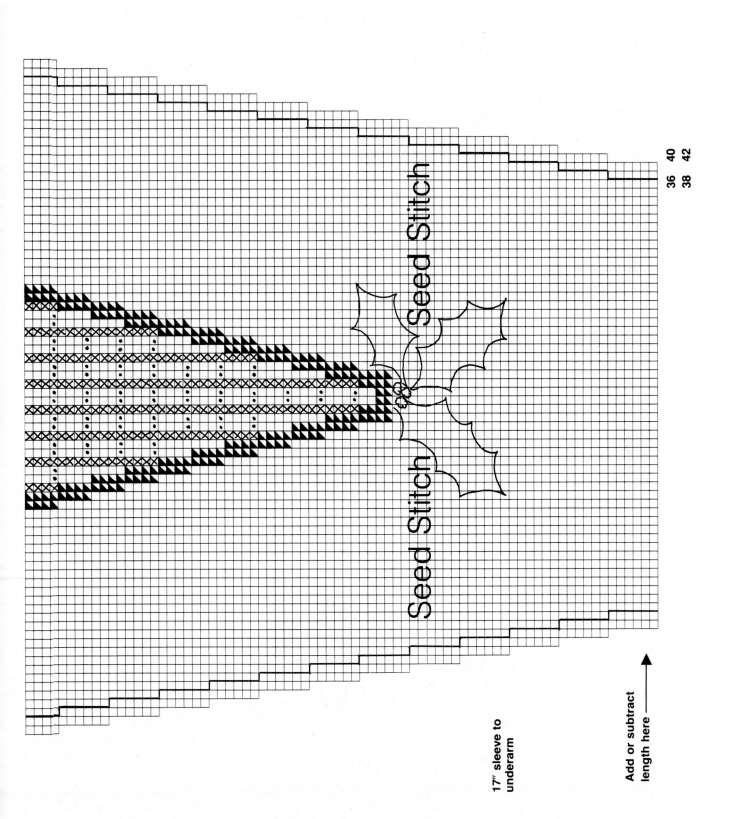

Seed Stitch

Seed Stitch

17" sleeve to
underarm

Add or subtract
length here ⟶

36 40
38 42

THE FERRY RIDE

Perhaps every small town has some equivalent of the North Haven ferry ride. The island resident setting out on any sort of journey must first spend an hour and ten minutes on a ninety-foot-long boat that carries nine cars on the deck. There is also a cabin, usually under- or over-heated, that seats thirty-five passengers, but often many more. The boat carries us twelve miles across a bay that can get very rough when high winds blow. These can be a common occurrence in the winter, often forcing the captain to cancel the trip and putting everyone's plans on hold until the next day.

When the captain decides that there will be no boat on a certain day, no one leaves. No one can override the captain's decision, and no amount of money or persuasion can change his mind. Business meetings, however important, must be canceled, flights must be missed, and even the dentist can be skipped when the winds blow. Ferry cancellations remind us that some forces, such as the weather, make the decisions for all of us and that there are limits to our control.

But when the ferry is running, it is more than mere transportation. The ferry is also a social gathering place, sparring ground, and common denominator for all of us who live on the island. Almost no one makes the ride daily to commute to a mainland job, but most of us ride the boat at least twice a month for doctors' appointments, shopping, and excursions.

Politics, child-rearing, small talk, hopes and dreams—you never know what will be discussed when you walk aboard. The ten-by-thirty-foot cabin is sometimes overcrowded, occasionally empty, and the mood inside can be as different as the weather outside. It is where the friend and foe must occasionally share a seat and engage in a conversation each thought impossible.

Walking in and taking a look around sometimes provides a clue to the tone of the day's ride. Are mothers gathered with a group of toddlers, providing snacks and readying plastic bags in case the trip is rougher than expected? Perhaps it is a different crowd and town meeting is drawing near—they'll be discussing the candidates for the school board and their spending records. Or perhaps a group composed mostly of men is monopolizing the coffee machine in the rear of the cabin, their backs plastered to the "head" doors, forcing others to squeeze through if they need to use the facilities. They might be comparing notes on road conditions, especially if it is spring and the frost heaves are beginning to surprise the unsuspecting driver.

Often, on entering, you see an empty seat next to the one person you have been meaning to talk to for the past month—and now you have an hour and a quarter to do so. It may be that you have a job that needs doing—painting your front hall or plowing your driveway next winter—or perhaps you've been asked to rototill a garden for the person, and this is a good chance to get the details of where to put it. Maybe you won't talk about a job at all, but rather about a personal problem. Your companion might be

an older parent who can offer some advice about those budding teenagers in your home, or it could be a peer who wants to discuss how you like the new teacher or if you have any ideas on how to get her husband to help with the dishes.

Or it can just as easily happen that the only empty seat is in front of the one person you have been avoiding ever since the school board meeting when you took opposite sides over changing the bus routes. It has been a couple months, and you're still not too sure how she feels about you, but you know it would look strange to stand the whole way on a trip that promises to be rough. After taking a deep breath, you stroll up to the seat and sit down. Just to test the waters you turn around and ask the one question that is always proper on the ferry ride, "Going over for the day?"

Before you know it, you've heard how many dentist appointments she and the kids have had in the past few months, and you've both discussed the merits of braces, sealants on the kids' teeth, and which dentist has better magazines in the waiting room. This in turn leads to talk about raising teenagers, marriage, and the future of the town. Another reminder that those things that we dread are never as bad as we think, and however divided we may seem at times, we are all basically the same. Handy lessons for just one hour and ten minutes on a boat.

Every ride is different—some too short, others endless; some crowded, others empty; some noisy, some quiet. Some are good for conversation, others for reading a book. People are usually more talkative in the morning on the way over and more pensive on the return—reading, napping, thinking over their day. The one universal factor is that we all must ride sometime, we all spend time in the cabin once in a while, and, even if only for that time, we are all interwoven in the fabric of our community.

WINDOW BOX PULLOVER

Sizes: 36 (38, 40)
Finished sizes: 38 (40, 42)"
Needles:
  Size 5 and 8 or size needed to obtain stitch gauge of 41/2 sts = 1" using larger needles over stockinette stitch
  Size 5 16" circular needle
Materials:
  7 4 oz skeins Main Color (MC) 50% Cotton/50% Wool worsted weight yarn (1120 yds)
  10 yds White
  30 yds Red Heather
  60 yds Pale Gray
  10 yds Green
  10 yds Plum
  10 yds Yellow
  10 yds Light Pink
  40 yds Blue

☐ NOTES

1. The large flowers are the only part of the "foliage" that is knit in.
2. Use a bobbin for each side of the "window frame" rather than carry the yarn across the back.
3. Do not follow chart design on back; rather, have a few "clapboards" at random, or nothing at all.

☐ PATTERN STITCH

Large Flower – on the right side, using the color for the large flower, K in front, then in back, then in front, then in back of the same stitch, 4 sts on needle. Turn, P4, turn, K2 tog in back, K2 tog in front, turn, P2 tog, turn, K the one st left with the background color and continue on. As you can see, bits of the MC can be seen in the flower. On the next row, purl the 2 sts that will become large flowers on the next row, using the flower color.

☐ FRONT

With smaller needles and MC, cast on 76 (80, 84) sts. Work in K1, P1 ribbing for 31/4", inc 10 sts evenly spaced in last row of ribbing — 86 (90, 94) sts. Change to larger needles and work 4 (8, 8) rows stockinette st. Right side facing, **begin body chart**. *Armhole shaping:* At beg of next 2 rows, bind off 6 sts. Dec 1 st each end of needle every other row 7 times. Work until armhole measures 51/2". Right side facing, work 21 (22, 23) sts, place center 18 (20, 22) sts on holder, join another ball of yarn, work to end. Dec 1 st at each neck edge every other row 4 (4, 5) times. Work until armhole measures 71/2 (71/2, 8)". Place shoulder sts on holders.

☐ BACK

Work as for Front except neck shaping. Place shoulder and 26 (28, 32) back neck sts on holders.

☐ SLEEVES

With smaller needles and MC, cast on 38 (40, 42) sts. Work K1, P1 ribbing for 31/4", inc 4 sts in the last row of ribbing. Change to larger needles and work 6 rows stockinette st and then work design of smaller "window box" (see chart) on one sleeve. **At the same time**, inc 1 st each end of needle every 8th row 7 times. Work until sleeve measures 161/2 (161/2, 17)" or desired length to underarm. At beg next 2 rows, bind off 6 sts. Dec 1 st each end of needle every other row 12 (13, 14) times — 20 sts. Dec 1 st each end of needle *every* row 12 times. Bind off rem 8 sts.

☐ FINISHING

Place shoulder sts of Front and Back right sides together. Using a third needle, knit the shoulders together and bind off the sts. With smaller circular needle, pick up and K72 (76, 80) sts around neck including sts on holders. Work in K1, P1 ribbing for 1". Bind off loosely so sweater will go over the head easily. Set in sleeves, sew rem seams, weave in all ends.

Chart for Front

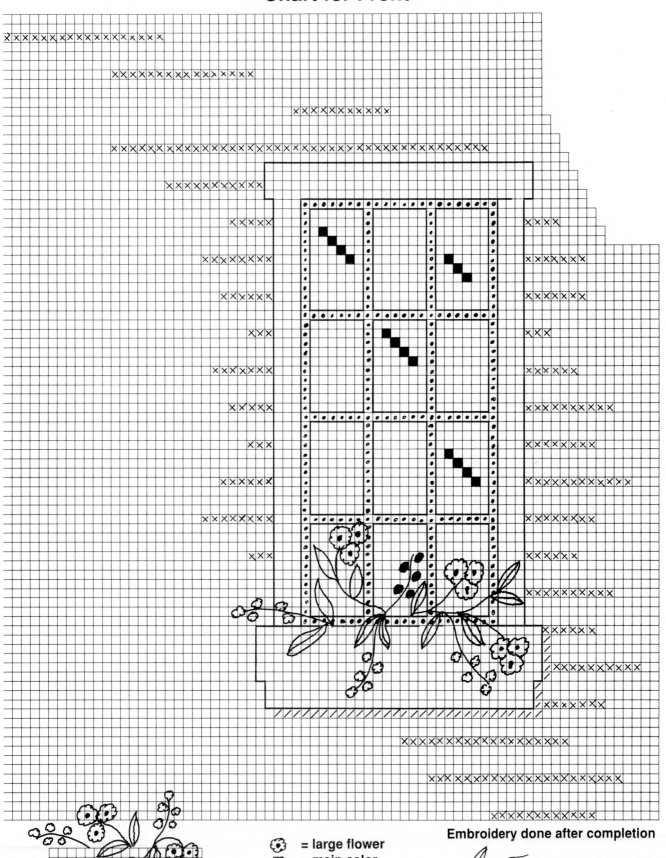

= large flower

= main color

= purl stitch

= shadow

= reflections

Embroidery done after completion

◀ lazy daisy

◀ outline stitch

◀ French knot

WINDOW BOX FOR ONE SLEEVE

Window Box Pullover

Ribbon Pullover

RIBBON PULLOVER

Sizes: 36 (38, 40)
Finished Sizes: 37³/4 (39¹/2, 41¹/4)"
Length to underarm: 15 (15¹/2, 16)"
Needles:
    Size 5 and 8 or size needed to obtain stitch
    gauge of 4¹/2 sts and 6 rows = 1" using
    larger needle over stockinette stitch
    Size 5 circular needle
Materials:
    7 3¹/2 oz skeins Main Color (MC) 50%
    Cotton/50% Wool
    60 yds Ribbon Color
    40 yds Contrasting Ribbon Color
    10 yds Pink
    10 yds Green

☐ NOTES

Any alteration in sweater length must be
made before beginning ribbon design.

☐ FRONT

With smaller needles and MC, cast on 82
(86, 90) sts. Work K1, P1 ribbing for 22 rows
(approx 3"), inc 3 sts evenly spaced across
last row of ribbing. Change to larger needles.
K1 row, P1 row. Next row K3 (5, 1), *slip 1,
K5, repeat from * across row, ending with K3
(5, 1). Purl back. Repeat these 2 rows for 32
(34, 36) rows above ribbing. **Start chart for
design.** Place center st on holder 2 rows
before armhole shaping. Join another ball of
yarn and work both sides at the same time.
Armhole shaping: At beg of next 2 rows, bind
off 6 sts. Dec 1 st at each end of needle every
other row 7 times **and at the same time** work
neck decs as follows: dec 1 st at neck edge
every 4th row 12 times. Slip shoulders sts to
holder, to be knit together with back
shoulder sts.

☐ BACK

Work same as front until armhole decs have
been completed. **Start chart for design.**
Work to completion of chart. *Shoulders:*
Holding Front and Back right sides together
and using a third needle, knit shoulders
together and bind off sts, working from
armhole edge toward neck. Place back neck
sts on holder.

☐ SLEEVES

With smaller needles and MC, cast on 40
(40, 42) sts. Work ribbing as for front, inc 5
(7, 7) sts evenly across last row. Change to
larger needles. Knit 1 row, purl 1 row. Next
row: K4 (5, 6), *slip 1, K5. Rep from * across
row ending K4 (5, 6). Purl back. Continue in
established patterns inc 1 st each end of
needle every 8th row 6 times. Work even
until sleeve measures 16 (16¹/2, 16¹/2)" or
desired length to underarm. *Sleeve cap:* At
beg of next 2 rows, bind off 6 sts. Dec 1 st
each end of needle every other row until 21
sts remain. Bind off 3 sts at beg of next 4
rows. Bind off remaining sts.

☐ NECK

With smaller circular needle and MC, right
side facing, knit back neck sts, pick up and
knit every 3 out of 4 available sts along neck
edge (approx 32–34 sts each side), and center
st on holder. Work K1, P1 ribbing, keeping
the one st at base of neck a K st and dec 1 st
each side of that center st every other row for
1". Bind off using a larger needle.

☐ FINISHING

Press all pieces before sewing together. Sew
side seams and sleeve seams by holding pieces
right sides together and using a backstitch.
Turn body wrong side out, sleeve right side
out. Place sleeve cap in armhole right sides
together, matching underarm and shoulders.
Sew together using backstitch, easing sleeve
cap to fit. Weave in all ends and press seams.
Embroider flowers and leaves as shown on
chart.

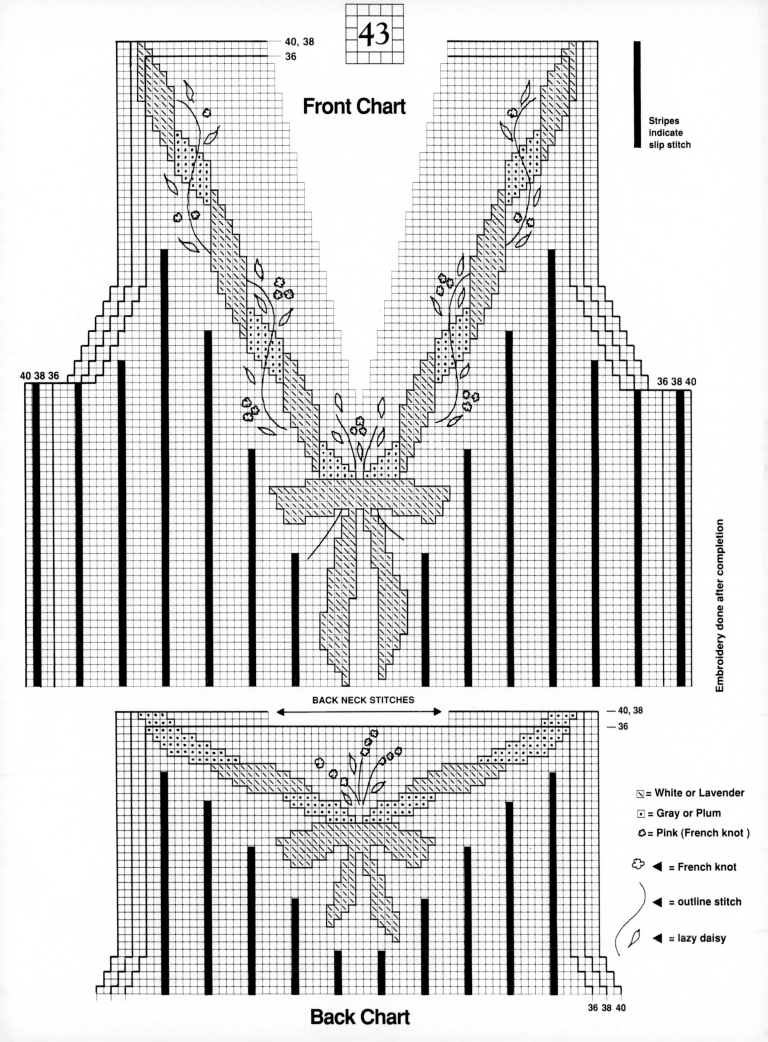

43

Front Chart

40, 38
36

Stripes indicate slip stitch

40 38 36

36 38 40

Embroidery done after completion

BACK NECK STITCHES

— 40, 38
— 36

⊠ = White or Lavender

⊡ = Gray or Plum

✿ = Pink (French knot)

✿ ◄ = French knot

◄ = outline stitch

◄ = lazy daisy

36 38 40

Back Chart

Loon Pullover

LOON

We decided to create a loon sweater because these beautiful birds are a cherished part of our lives. Anyone who has heard their mournful cry or seen their striking summer plumage can never forget them. While researching their coloring, we discovered to our sorrow that the loon's recent history reflects in microcosm human beings' relationship with the larger environment.

The common loon, *Gavia immer*, is considered to be the oldest bird in North America and one of the oldest birds on earth. Loons have existed for sixty million years. Nesting on northern lakes in the spring and traveling to salt water or large lakes in the winter, these birds cover a territory that ranges from Alaska to Florida and Mexico.

Often called the "great northern diver," the loon is well adapted to an aquatic way of life. It can dive as deep as two hundred feet to seize its prey, staying submerged for as long as three minutes. Its favorite foods include fish, mollusks, frogs, and aquatic insects. The loon's body is so highly specialized for diving that it has lost some of its ability to walk on land. The loon's webbed feet are set far back on its body, so that to wobble along on dry land it must also use its wings and bill. For this reason the loon nests close to the shore, virtually on the edge of the water, to avoid any walking.

The loon prefers to nest on an island in a lake but will also choose an open span of shore, thus forcing its land predators (raccoon, mink, beaver) to expose themselves as they approach. Their nests are fairly simple: usually a flattened scrape on the land lined with aquatic vegetation. The loon lays only two brown eggs to a nest, which means she can't afford to lose any.

Although the species is ancient, loons seem to have fairly modern attitudes toward rearing their young. Both parents tend the nest throughout the incubation process, which lasts twenty-six to twenty-nine days. If the eggs survive unharmed, the hatched chicks are dark charcoal-gray with a lighter breast. The parents are very attentive to their young, swimming around them and carrying them on their backs. Riding on the back serves two purposes. The first is to protect the chicks from large fish and snapping turtles who would pull them down into the water. Brooding is the second, since loons rarely return to the nest once the chicks are hatched. The feathers under a chick's wings are sparse. The chick keeps warm and dry riding on its parent's back.

The name *loon* is related to the Old Norse word for *lament*, which refers to the wail that one loon uses to locate another. The wail is often heard at night when one loon is ready to pass on nest duties to its mate. The characteristic laughing cry, known as a tremolo, is used to indicate alarm, usually at a disturbance caused by a human, a natural predator, or another loon. The tremolo consists of three to ten notes uttered rapidly and evenly—a sound I used to try to imitate as a child. Standing by the side of the water, I would cry out to loons in the evening and usually get an answer.

These stunning birds now face multiple dangers, and their numbers have dwindled considerably over the years. Natural predators have always been a problem, but raccoons and skunks have become particularly troublesome in populated areas, where they can find abundant food from family garbage cans and dumps and have no significant enemies.

Humankind has been the loon's greatest enemy since the 1800s when loons were routinely shot just because they were suspected of competing with humans for the fish in newly settled lake regions. (Actually, most of the fish that loons catch are smaller than those of interest to fishermen.) In the early 1900s when indiscriminate sport shooting along the flyways brought down

Continued on page 96

LOON PULLOVER

Sizes: 34 (38, 42)
Finished Sizes: 36 (40, 44)"
Needles:
  Size 5 and 8 24" circular needles or size
  needed to obtain stitch gauge of 41/2 sts =
  1" using larger needles over stockinette
  stitch
  Size 8 16" circular needle
  Size 5 and 8 double pointed needles (dpn)
Materials:
  5 4 oz skeins Midnight (MC) worsted
  weight yarn (1000 yds)
  1 4oz skein White worsted weight yarn
  (200 yds)
  50 yds Black worsted weight yarn
  50 yds Black fingering yarn
  1 Loon button
  1 Pewter clasp

☐ NOTES

Body is worked in the round to the underarms and then divided. Front and Back are worked separately back and forth following graphs to the shoulder. Sleeves are worked in the round to the underarm and then worked back and forth following graphs to the shoulder. The sleeve pattern ends at the shoulder and the saddle shoulder is continued in MC.

☐ BODY

With smaller 24" circular needle and Black, cast on 140 (160, 180) sts. Join and place marker. Work one rnd in K1, P1 ribbing. Change to MC and work 20 rnds ribbing. Inc 20 sts evenly across last rnd of ribbing — 160 (180, 200) sts. Change to larger 24" circular needle and **begin Chart A**. Rep last 4 rows of Chart A 14 times (approx 151/2") or work desired length to underarm ending 5 (6, 7) sts before marker. Place next 10 (12, 14) sts on holder for left underarm. Divide for Front and Back.

☐ BACK

Turn, following chart, purl across 70 (78, 86) sts, place next 10 (12, 14) sts on holder for right underarm. Place rem 70 (78, 86) sts on holder for Front and work on Back sts only. Working back and forth, follow Back chart working dec every other row 5 times. Work to end of chart following correct size. Leave sts on spare needle.

☐ FRONT

Put Front sts on holder on larger needle. Wrong side facing, join yarn at right underarm, purl and follow Front chart working dec every other row 5 times. Join a second ball of yarn at placket marking and work both sides of Front at the same time. Work to end of chart following correct size. Leave sts on spare needle.

☐ SLEEVES

With smaller dpn and Black, cast on 40 sts. Join and place marker. Work one rnd K1, P1 ribbing. Change to MC and work 20 rnds in ribbing. Increase 5 (15, 15) sts evenly across last row of ribbing. Change to larger dpn and **begin Chart A**. Increase 1 st each side of marker (begin after first rep of Chart A) every 8 rnds 7 (5, 8) times — 59 (65, 71) sts. Rep last 4 rows of Chart A until piece measures 16 (17, 171/2)" from beg, or desired length to underarm ending 5 (6, 7) sts before marker. Place next 10 (12, 14) sts on holder for underarm. Turn, work back and forth following Sleeve chart shaping to end of chart following correct size. 13 sts remain for saddle.

☐ RIGHT SADDLE

With right side facing, *K12, Sl 1, K2 tog from right back, pass slip st over knit st (PSSO), turn, P12, Sl 1, P2 tog from right front, PSSO, turn*, work * to * until all the shoulder sts on each side are worked in — 16 (18, 20) sts remain on Front. Turn, K12, Sl 1, K2 tog, PSSO, and then continue around back neck sts to other shoulder. Rep for other sleeve.

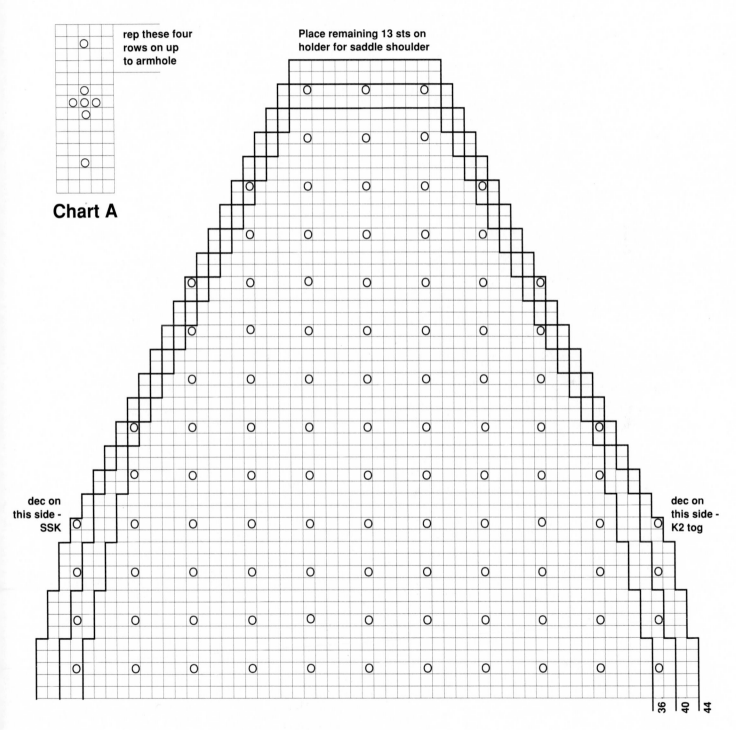

Chart A

rep these four
rows on up
to armhole

Place remaining 13 sts on
holder for saddle shoulder

dec on
this side -
SSK

dec on
this side -
K2 tog

36 40 44

Chart for Sleeve

LOON PULLOVER

☐ NECK

Right side facing with smaller 16" circular needle, attach Black. K15 (17, 19), K2 tog, K12, Sl 1, K1, PSSO, K29 (33, 37), K2 tog, K13, Sl 1, K1, PSSO, K15 (17, 19) — 87 (95, 103) sts. *Dec row:* P16 (18, 20), [P2 tog, P2] 3 times, P2 tog, P29 (33, 37), P2 tog, [P2, P2 tog] 3 times, P15 (17, 19) — 75 (87, 95) sts. Next row, *K1 Black, K1 White across row, end K1 Black. Turn, P1 Black, P1 White across row, end P1 Black. Rep from * once. Work 2 rows Black. Leave sts on needle.

☐ FINISHING

Wrong side facing, with 2 smaller dpn and double-strand Black fingering yarn, cast on 3 sts. K in back of first st of neck at base of placket, pass last st of cast-on sts over this st. *Slide sts to right end of needle, K2, Sl 1 as if to purl, knit in back of next st, PSSO*, work * to *. Work up left side of placket, knit one extra row either side of corner st to get a nice square corner, work around neck and down right front to beginning of placket. Bind off 3 sts. Graft underarm sts. Sew sleeves to body. Sew on loon button and clasp. Weave in ends.

☐ GRAFTING

Place underarm sts on dpn. With an equal number of sts on each needle, begin with the first st on right-hand end of front needle. Bring tapestry needle, threaded with a long piece of MC, through the front st purlwise, leaving it on the needle. Poke tapestry needle through back st as if to knit. Bring tapestry needle through the front st as if to knit and slip this st off the needle. Bring tapestry needle through next front st as if to purl, leaving it on the needle. Slip the back st off the needle, purlwise, and then bring the tapestry needle through the next back st as if to knit, leaving it on the needle. The grafting yarn becomes another row of knitting. Continue until all sts are secure.

LOON PULLOVER

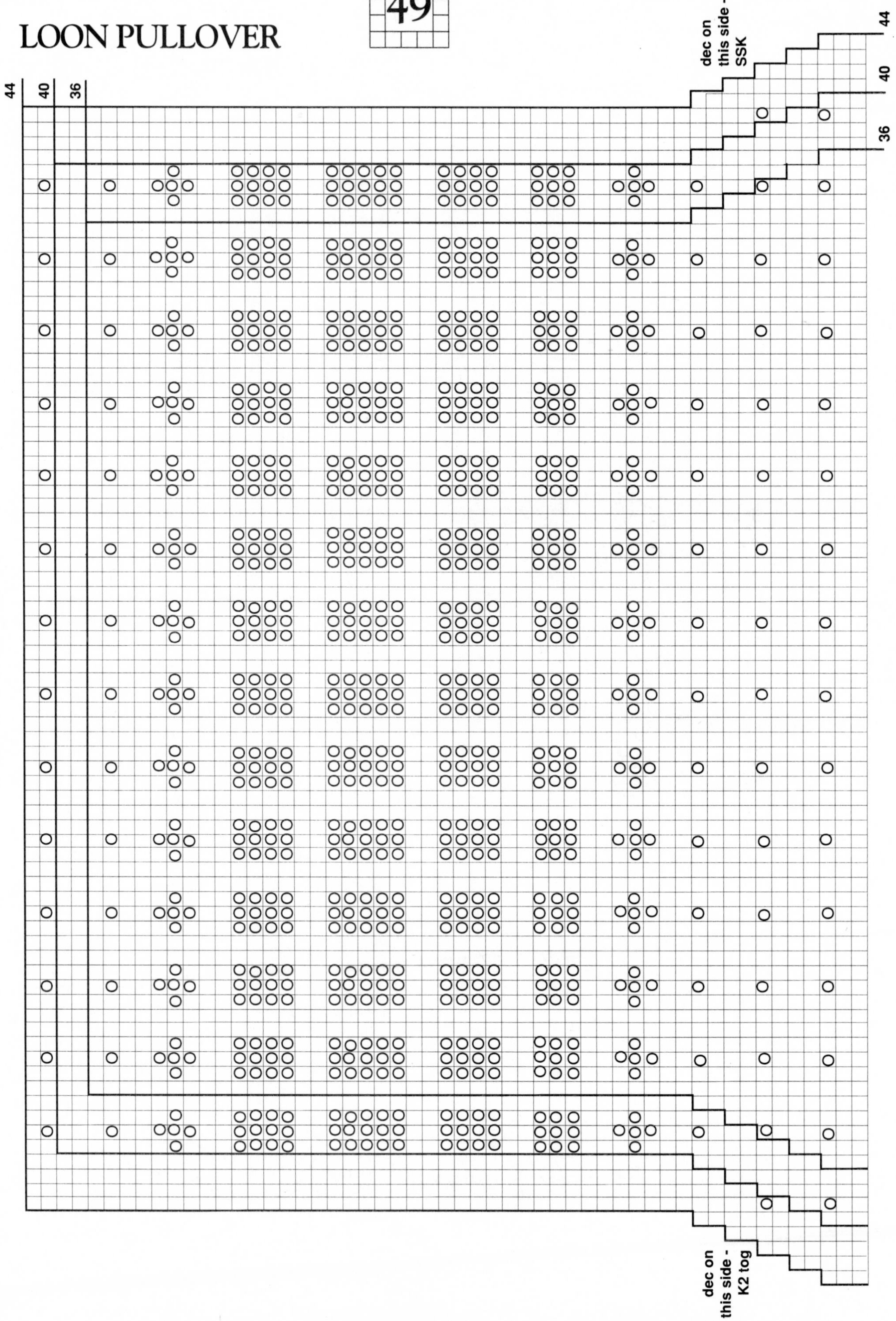

Chart for Back

44 40 36

44

dec on this side - SSK

44 40 36

dec on this side - K2 tog

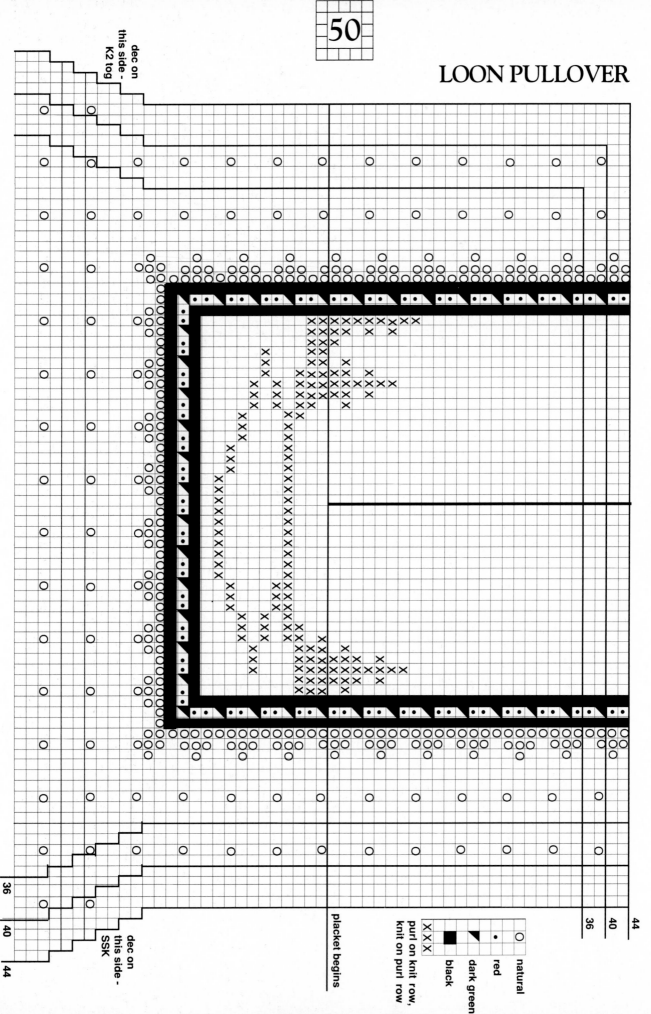

50

LOON PULLOVER

Chart for Front

dec on this side - K2 tog

dec on this side - SSK

placket begins

○	natural
•	red
◼	dark green
◼	black

purl on knit row,
knit on purl row

X X X	

purl on knit row, knit on purl row

GRAPE PULLOVER

Chart for Back and Front

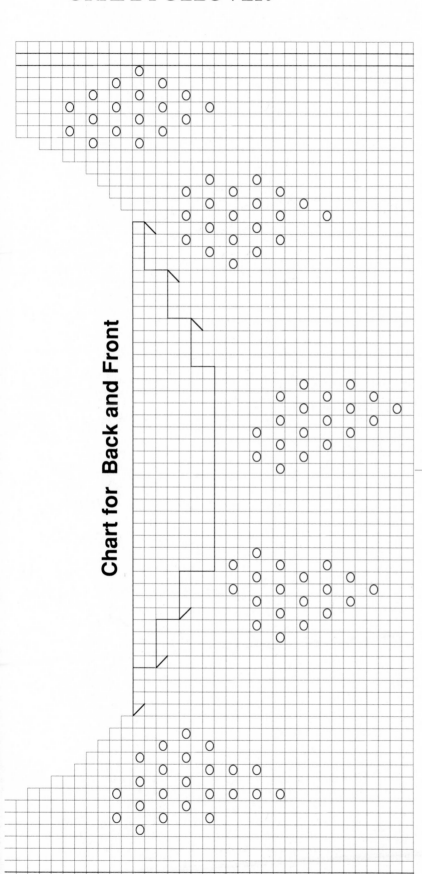

Center stitch for Back and Front

Chart for Sleeves

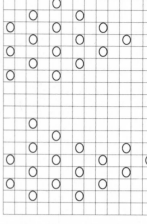

Center stitch of Sleeve

○ = Knit the stitch using grape color, stitch is now on right needle. Insert left hand needle in front of stitch and then knit the stitch again, then knit in front and back and front and back and front (six loops of grape color on right needle). Slip 5 of the loops over one as if binding off until one loop is left. Bring bobble around to front of work. Knit next stitch in background color.

◩ = Purl 2 sts together

◪ = Slip next 2 sts singly as if to knit to right hand needle. Place tip of left hand needle through both loops and knit together.

Grape Pullover

SMALL TALK

Small talk is a constant and comforting part of our island's life. With it you can establish a connection with almost anyone, regardless of political or philosophical beliefs. Small talk addresses that which we all have in common.

The weather is high on the list of everyone's favorite small-talk topics, and the island is one of those places where it actually matters. In windy weather our ferry doesn't travel, or if it does, those travelers with weak stomachs or deep fears have a decision to make. Hence, the day before a planned trip, a traveler may ask a number of residents for their predictions about the coming day's weather. In very cold weather with no wind, ice can block the harbor or lengthen the trip while the icebreaker works its way through.

Hot weather is as good a topic as cold, damp as good as dry, but many other suitable topics for noncommittal small talk exist. A person's health brings up the health of others ("I just got over this mess that is going around town"). Perhaps you and another experience the same cold symptoms or have the same remedy for a headache. Small talk about our health provides us with another opportunity to find a common bond.

Experienced small-talkers, those who have braved the topic of health, will tackle more advanced inconsequential talk. Queries about relatives or about recent travels or events can easily lead to conversation that stays within the realm of the noncommittal and noncontroversial.

We not only have many "small" topics from which to choose, we also have many places to conduct such talk. The pace of life is often much slower on an island, especially in the winter. And even in the summer, when life is too hurried, we deliberately use conversation to slow it down.

A short walk through town can produce a discussion of the weather with the postmaster, a collection of opinions on why the ferry is late as you pass through the parking lot at the landing, a talk with the store clerk about her rabbits, and a few words about business at the ice cream stand. Then there are all the people you will meet on the street. In the summer you won't know them all, but of those you do, many will be on vacation and will want to exchange a few words with you. If they are used to a faster pace, they may be eager to brush up on their inconsequential-conversation skills. All this occurs during the span of time intended for mailing a letter, which, as my co-workers have learned to expect, can be a lengthy process.

In other places especially, but even among ourselves, there are those who consider small talk a great waste of time. What, then, is its appeal, and, even more important, its significance? For me it provides a necessary link to my fellow earth-mates. It's an opportunity to let myself off the hook, to be average, to simply enjoy the many things we all have in common instead of looking for the differences.

GRAPE PULLOVER

Sizes: 34 (36, 38)
Finished Sizes: 36 (38, 40)"
Needles:
    Size 4 and 7 or size needed to obtain stitch gauge of 5 sts = 1" using larger needles over stockinette stitch
    Size 4 and 7 16" circular needles
    Stitch holders and cable needle (cn)
Materials:
    5 (5, 6) 4 oz skeins Main Color (MC) worsted weight yarn (1000–1200 yds)
    120 yds Plum worsted weight yarn
    100 yds Green fingering yarn (use double)
    10 yds Brown fingering yarn

☐ **PATTERN STITCHES**
LT (Left Twist) – Skip 1 st, knit 2nd st through back loop, then knit skipped st.
RT (Right Twist) – Skip 1 st, knit 2nd st, then knit the skipped st.
TW3 – Slip next 2 sts onto cn and hold at back of work, K1, slip 2 sts on cn to left hand needle and work LT.

☐ **BACK**
With smaller needles and MC, cast on 85 (89, 93) sts. Work cable ribbing as follows:
Row 1 (right side): K1 (edge st), K0 (0, 1), P0 (0, 1), K0 (2, 2), *P1, K1, P1, K2*, work * to *, end P1, K1, P1, K0 (2, 2), P0 (0, 1), K0 (0, 1), K1 (edge st).
Rows 2 and 4: Knit the knit sts and purl the purl sts. *Row 3:* K1, K0 (0, 1), P0 (0, 1), RT0 (1, 1), *P1, K1, P1, RT*, work * to *, end P1, K1, P1, RT0 (1, 1), P0 (0, 1), K0 (0, 1), K1.
Rep these 4 rows for rib pattern. Work sts as established for approx 5", end with right-side row. Wrong side facing, work inc row as follows: P7 (9, 11), *inc 1 in next st by purling in back and front strands of st, P9*, work * to * 7 times total, inc 1, P7 (9, 11) sts — 93 (97, 101) sts.
Sizes 36 (38) only: Change to larger needles.
Row 1: K6 (8), *RT, LT, K7*, work * to * end K6 (8).
Row 2 and all even-numbered rows: Purl.
Row 3: K5 (7), *RT, K2, LT, K5*, work * to *, end K5 (7).
Row 5: K4 (6), *RT, K4, LT, K3*, work

* to *, end K4 (6).
Row 7: K3 (5), *RT, K6, LT, K1*, work * to *, end K3 (5).
Row 9: K12 (14), *TW3, K8*, work *, to *, end K12 (14).
Row 11: K3 (5), *LT, K6, RT, K1*, work * to *, end K3 (5).
Row 13: K4 (6), *LT, K4, RT, K3*, work * to *, end K4 (6).
Row 15: K5 (7), *LT, K2, RT, K5*, work * to *, end K5 (7).
Row 17: K6 (8), *LT, RT, K7*, work * to *, end K6 (8).
Row 19: K6 (8), *P1, RT, P1, K7*, work * to *, end K6 (8).
Row 20 and all following rows: Work sts as established, crossing cables as on Row 19 every 4th row.
Size 40 only: Change to larger needles.
Row 1: K1, *LT, K7, RT*, work * to *, end K1.
Row 2 and all even-numbered rows: Purl.
Row 3: K2, *LT, K5, RT, K2*, work * to *.
Row 5: K3, *LT, K3, RT, K4*, work * to *, end K3.
Row 7: K4, *LT, K1, RT, K6*, work * to *, end K4.
Row 9: K5, *TW3, K8*, work * to *, end K5.
Row 11: K4, *RT, K1, LT, K6*, work * to *, end K4.
Row 13: K3, *RT, K3, LT, K4*, work * to *, end K3.
Row 15: K2, *RT, K5, LT, K2*, work * to *.
Row 17: K1, *RT, K7, LT*, work * to *, end K1.
Row 19: K10, *P1, RT, P1, K7*, work * to *, end K10.
Row 20 and all following rows: Work sts as established, crossing cables as on Row 19 every 4th row. Work until length to underarm is 13 1/2 (14, 141/2)" from beg. *Armhole shaping:* At beg of next 2 rows, bind off 8 sts. Dec 1 st each end of needle every other row 4 (5, 6) times — 69 (71, 73) sts. **At the same time,** after completing 9 (11, 12) cable crossings, work across 2 center cables (3rd and 4th cables on needle) in stockinette st. After 10 (12, 13) cable crossings, work across next 2 cables (2nd and 5th cables) in stockinette st. After 12 (14, 15) cable crossings, work even in stockinette st **and at**

the same time, 4 rows after completing 2 center cables, **begin chart** for placement of bobbles for grapes. (Leaves are knit separately and sewn on later.) Work even until piece measures 6" above armhole, end with wrong-side row.

Neck shaping: With right side facing, K14 (15, 16) sts, place center 41 sts on holder for neck, join another ball of MC and K14 (15, 16) sts. Working both sides at the same time, at each neck edge dec 1 st *every* row 5 times, then every other row 3 times. Bind off rem 6 (7, 8) sts on each shoulder.

☐ FRONT

Work Front same as Back until piece measures 5" above armhole. *Neck shaping:* K26 (27, 28) sts, place center 17 sts on holder. Join 2nd ball of MC and K26 (27, 28) sts. Working both sides at the same time, *at each neck edge, [bind off 3 sts once and dec 1 st once], every other row*, work * to * twice. Dec 1 st at neck edge *every* row 5 times. Dec 1 st at neck edge every other row 3 times, bind off rem 6 (7, 8) sts on each shoulder.

☐ SLEEVE

With smaller needles and MC, cast on 45 sts and work in cable ribbing as follows: K1, *P1, K1, P1, K2*, work * to * 8 times total, end with P1, K1, P1, K1. Work in cable rib as on back for approx 3 1/2", end with right side row. Wrong side facing, work inc row as follows: P7, *inc 1 in next st, P9*, work * to * 3 times total, inc 1 in next st, P7 sts — 49 sts. Change to larger needles and continue in pattern st as on back, inc 1 st at each end of needle every 6th row 9 (11, 13) times — 67 (71, 75) sts. Work new sts in stockinette st. After 16 (18, 19) cable crossings work across 2 center cables in stockinette st. After 17 (19, 20) cable crossings work even in stockinette st **and at the same time**, 4 rows after completing 2 center cables, **begin chart** for placement of bobbles for grapes. Work until piece measures 16 (17, 17 1/2)" from beg or desired length. *Sleeve cap:* At beg of next 2 rows, bind off 7 sts. Dec 1 st at each edge every other row 12 (13, 14) times. Bind off 3

sts at beg of next 6 rows. Bind off rem 11 (13, 15) sts.

☐ FINISHING

Sew shoulder seams. With larger circular needles and MC, pick up and K135 (140, 145) sts around neck, including sts on holders. Work 3 rnds as follows: *P1, K1, P1, K2*, work * to * around. Work next rnd as follows: *P1, K1, P1, RT*, work * to * around. Change to smaller circular needle, rep the last 4 rnds, then work first 3 rnds again. Dec rnd: *Sl 1, P2 tog, PSSO, RT*, work * to * around 81 (84, 87) sts. Work 3 rnds as follows: *P1, K2*, work * to * around. Next rnd: *P1, RT*, work * to * around. Rep last 4 rnds once. Work 1 rnd of P1, K2 ribbing, bind off loosely.

☐ LEAVES

With smaller needles and Green (use double), cast on 3 sts.
Row 1: K1, inc 2 in next st as follows: K in back, front and back of st, K1.
Row 2: P2, Sl 1, P2.
Row 3: K2, inc 2 in next st, K2.
Row 4: P3, Sl 1, P3.
Row 5: K3, inc 2 in next st, K3.
Row 6: P4, Sl 1, P4.
Row 7: K4, inc 2 in next st, K4.
Row 8: P5, Sl 1, P5.
Row 9: K5, inc 2 in next st, K5.
Row 10: P6, Sl 1, P6.
Row 11: K6, inc 2 in next st, K6.
Row 12: Bind off 3 sts, P3, Sl 1, P7.
Row 13: Bind off 3 sts, K3, inc 2 in next st, K4.
Row 14: Bind off 3 sts, P1, Sl 1, P5.
Row 15: Bind off 3 sts, K1, inc 2 in next st, K2.
Row 16: Bind off 3 sts, P3.
Row 17: Bind off 3 sts, pull yarn through remaining st.
Break yarn, leaving tail to sew it on with. Make 16 leaves. Set in sleeves. Sew side and sleeve seams. Sew on leaves using photo as a guide. Embroider stems in outline st with Brown yarn. Press seams lightly.

Plum Peasant Vest

Teal Peasant Vest

PEASANT VEST

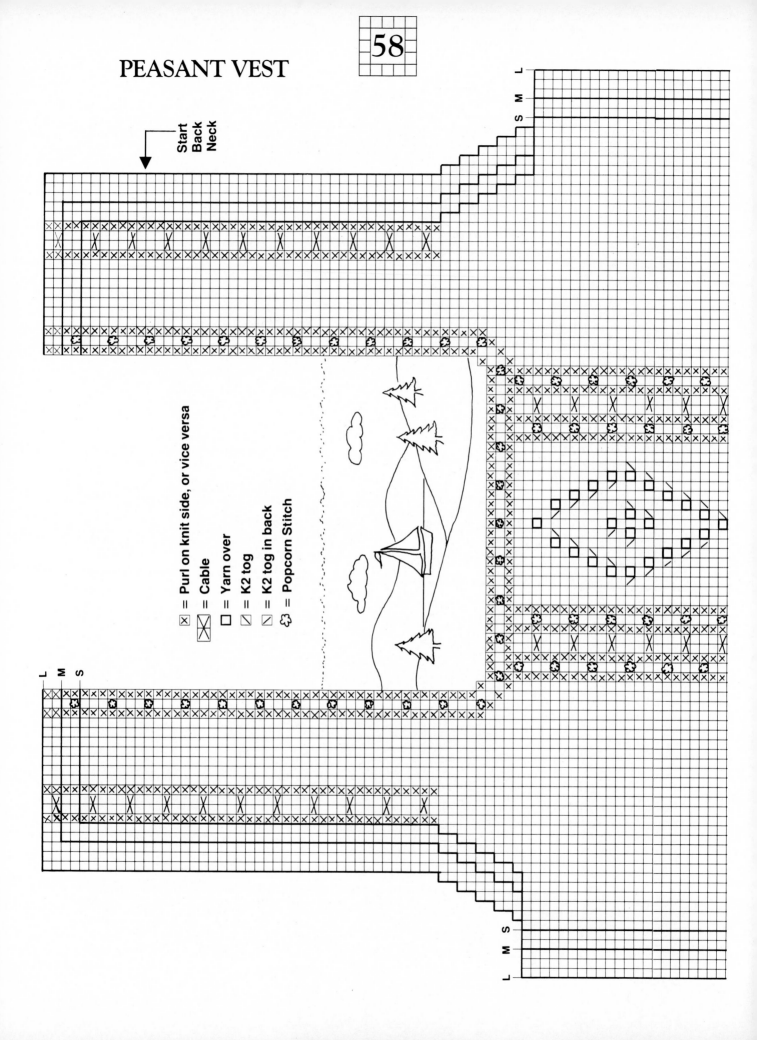

58

Start
Back
Neck

⊠ = Purl on knit side, or vice versa

◻◻ = Cable

☐ = Yarn over

◹ = K2 tog

◿ = K2 tog in back

❀ = Popcorn Stitch

S M L

L M S

S M L

L M S

59

White Peasant Vest

PEASANT VEST

Sizes: 36 (38, 40)
Finished Sizes: 38 (40, 42)"
Needles:
    Size 5 and 8 or size needed to obtain stitch
    gauge of 41/2 sts = 1" using larger needles
    over stockinette stitch
    Size 2 for inset
Materials:
    3 4 oz skeins (MC) worsted weight yarn
    (600 yds)
    50 yds Robin's Egg Blue fingering yarn
    (doubled)
    20 yds Medium Blue fingering yarn
    (doubled)
    20 yds Light Green fingering yarn
    (doubled)
    20 yds Medium Green fingering yarn
    (doubled)
    20 yds Dark Green fingering yarn
    (doubled)
    20 yds Lavender fingering yarn (doubled)
    20 yds White fingering yarn (doubled)
    5 yds Dark Brown fingering yarn (doubled)
    5 yds Pink fingering yarn (doubled)
    5 yds Purple fingering yarn (doubled)

☐ NOTES
After decreases at armhole edges have been
completed, work purl st and cable pattern on
4 stitches at armhole edge. (Only smallest size
placement of pattern is shown on graph.)

☐ PATTERN STITCHES
Popcorn Stitch: K1, P1, K1, P1, K1 in the
same stitch, then loop 4 sts over 1.
Mock Cable: Row 1: Skip 1 st, knit 2nd st,
then knit the skipped st. *Rows 2 and 4:* P2.
Row 3: K2.

☐ FRONT
With smaller needles and MC, cast on 79
(83, 89) sts. Follow chart for first 20 rows for
ribbing. Change to larger needles and
continue with chart adding sts at sides as
indicated. *Armhole shaping:* At beg of next 2
rows (Rows 83 & 84), bind off 6 sts. Dec 1 st
at each end of needle every other row 5
times. On Row 88 (a purl row), bind off
center 33 sts. On Row 89, dec 1 st at neck
edge. Join another ball of yarn, dec 1 st at
neck edge. Work both sides at the same time.
After decreases at armholes have been
completed, begin mock cable pattern. Follow
chart to end and place sts on holder to be
knit together with back sts.

☐ BACK
Work Back same as Front to armhole. Bind
off sts and work decs same as Front except
work 2 more triangles up back (5 in all), and
then work neck same as Front neck, working
Row 86 of Front at Row 126 on Back.

☐ FINISHING
Place shoulder sts on needles with right sides
together, with third needle knit sts from
Front and Back together and bind off at same
time. Sew remaining seams, weave in all
ends.

☐ INSET
With Size 2 needles and double strand of
fingering yarn, cast on 50 sts. **Work selected
chart**. Next row: *K2 tog, yarn over, rep
from * across row. Work 3 rows in stockinette
st, bind off, weave in all ends, fold and press
to create small hem. Hem with overcast
stitch on wrong side. Place inset in bodice
and stitch in place. Block.

PEASANT VEST

Wildflowers

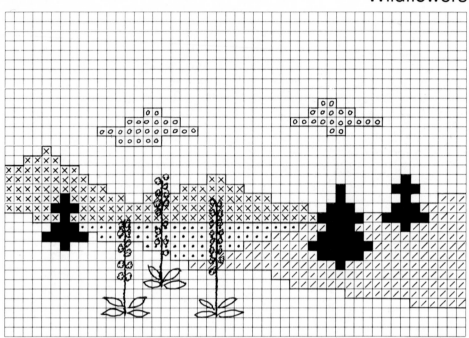

Sky = 25 yds Robin's Egg Blue

Field = 20 yds Medium Green

Flowers = Pink & Purple (French Knots)

⊘ = 10 yds Light Green

· = 10 yds Blue

☒ = 10 yds Lavender

■ = 10 yds Dark Green

◎ = 10 yds White

◪ = Dark Brown

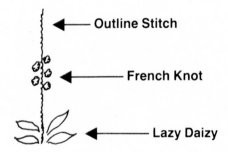

← Outline Stitch

← French Knot

← Lazy Daizy

PEASANT VEST

Sheep

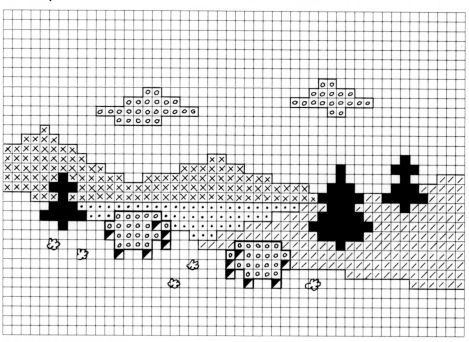

Sailboat

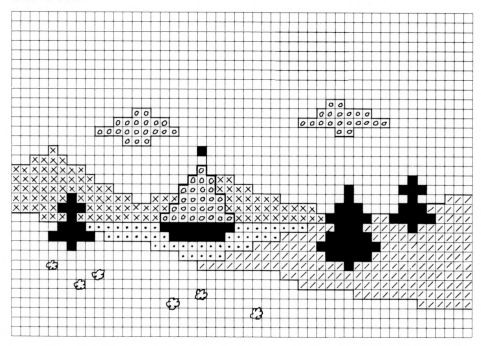

SIMPLE ENTERTAINMENT

One of the first questions I am asked when someone learns that I live on an island is. "What do you miss?" Going out to eat or the movies? Shopping or sports events? It would be dishonest to pretend that I don't miss those things at times. A houseful of kids on a cold rainy day reminds me that if we were somewhere else their father could take them to the movies. Nor am I immune to wishing that I could distract myself with a trip to the mall to look for that book I have been wanting to read or that new pair of shorts when I am faced with a stack of work on my desk.

But, regrets aside, most of the time I am just too busy to miss those things. Of course, in the summer the fast pace is no surprise to anyone. To begin with, most year-round residents work very hard during the summer, since that is when they earn most of their income. After work there are numerous activities: boating, picnicking, eating out at the seasonal eating places, shopping in the seasonal gift shops, visiting occasional art exhibits, concerts—a whole year's worth of culture and outdoor recreation packed into short months.

What about the other ten months? What do we do all winter? I think winter is when an appreciation of simple pleasures is important.

To hear old-timers talk, since the advent of television, homemade entertainment has been in decline. There used to be a lot of amateur musicians, even a local band, and more "fraternal" organizations. Gone are the Pythian Sisters, who were established on the island in 1911 and whose meeting hall is now our place of business. The Pythian Sisters were a secret society whose members were sworn to uphold many elevated principles, including the golden rule.

The past notwithstanding, I, as a member of the TV generation, am impressed with how much home-grown entertainment endures. Some of the traditional organizations such as the Grange (whose rituals focus on agriculture) have survived. The Grange welcomes everyone into its ranks, although a vote must be taken before a new member is admitted. Bimonthly meetings, except in the summmer, are attended by fifteen to thirty people and always include a potluck supper. Depending on the supper committee, the fare may be highly specialized or, my favorite, a free-for-all. Everyone is told to just bring "something"—this can result in all salads or all desserts.

Even better is when the Grange sponsors public suppers. These have a theme—beans, fish chowder, or casseroles. A group of men and women contribute their time to put the meal together—usually with donated food—and use the cash taken at the door to support the Grange. Public suppers are more sociable than restaurant meals. Everyone sits at long tables, and you never know who you will end up talking to—a teacher you have never gotten to know or an older person who has just the piece of information you were looking for. Because it is your friends and neighbors who are bringing out the food and coffee, there is always a lot of joking about rock-hard biscuits or extra helpings of pie.

Public suppers (or breakfasts or dinners—that's what people call a midday meal—or coffee hours) are not the special province of the Grange: they are often sponsored by the church or the Lion's Club. Even an enterprising group of kids trying to raise money will plan a public supper, put up the posters, cook, and clean up the mess. Lately the Grange suppers have been orchestrated by the men, clearly a reflection of the changing times.

I have to admit that a lot of the local entertainment is designed to spread the money around, and people are always trying to think up creative new schemes for fund-raising. Beano (bingo) is popular, but one of my personal favorites is the penny sale. This is complicated to explain but easy to play once you catch on. One purchases a card of tickets—fifty for one dollar (all right, maybe it should be called a two-penny sale). The bearer separates all the tickets from each other (an entertaining pastime in itself while chatting with the person in the next chair) and keeps the stub, with each ticket's number on it. While the participants are busy separating, the organizers are piling prizes on the table.

A word about the prizes: They have all been solicited from the community and can include such diverse items as home-baked bread, old paperback books, canned goods (the bing-cherry soup you never got around to eating), and kitchen utensils. The penny sale is a cross between a rummage sale and bake sale—two other popular pastimes. The goods are piled together in groups, with a few hot items placed together with the canned spinach and the old canisters. In front of each pile is a bowl into which anxious gamblers

place as many tickets as they wish. A plate of cream puffs will attract large numbers of tickets; a pile of old records will not draw as well.

When everyone has completed placing bids, the suspense mounts as the drawing begins. One number is chosen, and the holder of the number is awarded whatever is in the pile. Everyone manages to find great humor in the luck of certain repeat winners, and teasing and joking make the evening pass quickly. Refreshments are served, and there is always a door prize. It isn't the opera, and these performances don't win Academy Awards, but it is a lighthearted way to spend an evening with your kids and neighbors.

The island is a community with a diverse range of entertainment activities, and not all are for fund-raising. We have dances, gatherings with numerous kegs of beer, and summer beach parties that last half the night. But whatever people do in this town when they get together, they make the entertainment. People cook and invite each other over instead of going out to a restaurant. They drop by for a visit instead of going out to a football game or a movie. When feeling less sociable, people stay home and watch TV or take a drive alone to look at the sunset.

People create much of their own entertainment just by being involved with each other or talking to each other—at the store, waiting for the ferry, or out walking the dog. I find that it is hard to fit in all of the conversations, places to go, or people to visit or invite over for a meal. When people from mainland suburbs ask me what I do all winter, I can't help but wonder what they do without the entertainment of a small town.

ISLAND SPRUCE CARDIGAN

Lengthen or shorten here

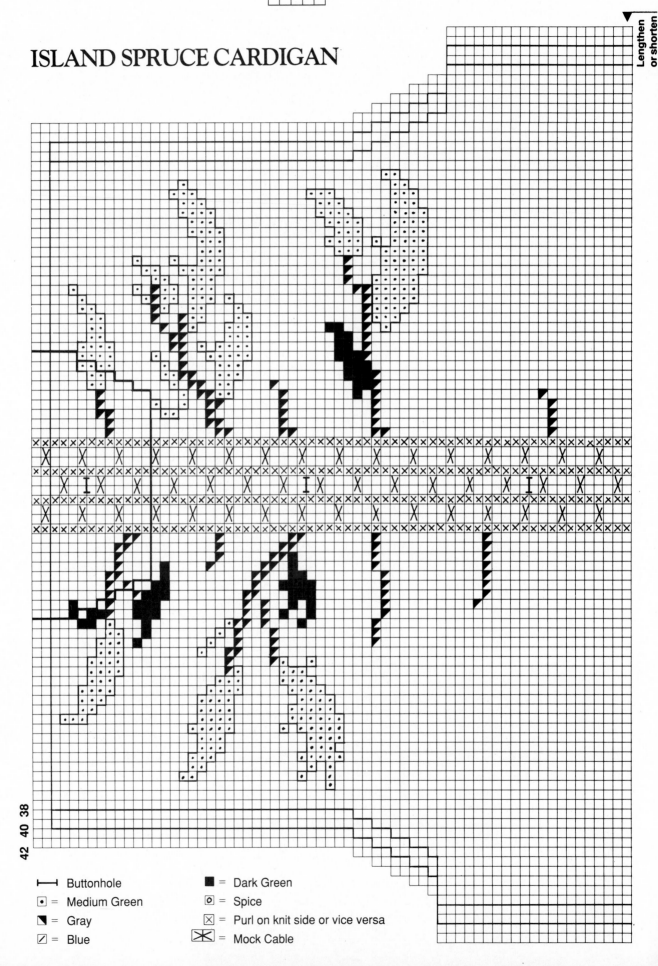

42 40 38

⊢─ Buttonhole		■ = Dark Green
⊡ = Medium Green		⊙ = Spice
◣ = Gray		⊠ = Purl on knit side or vice versa
⊘ = Blue		⋈ = Mock Cable

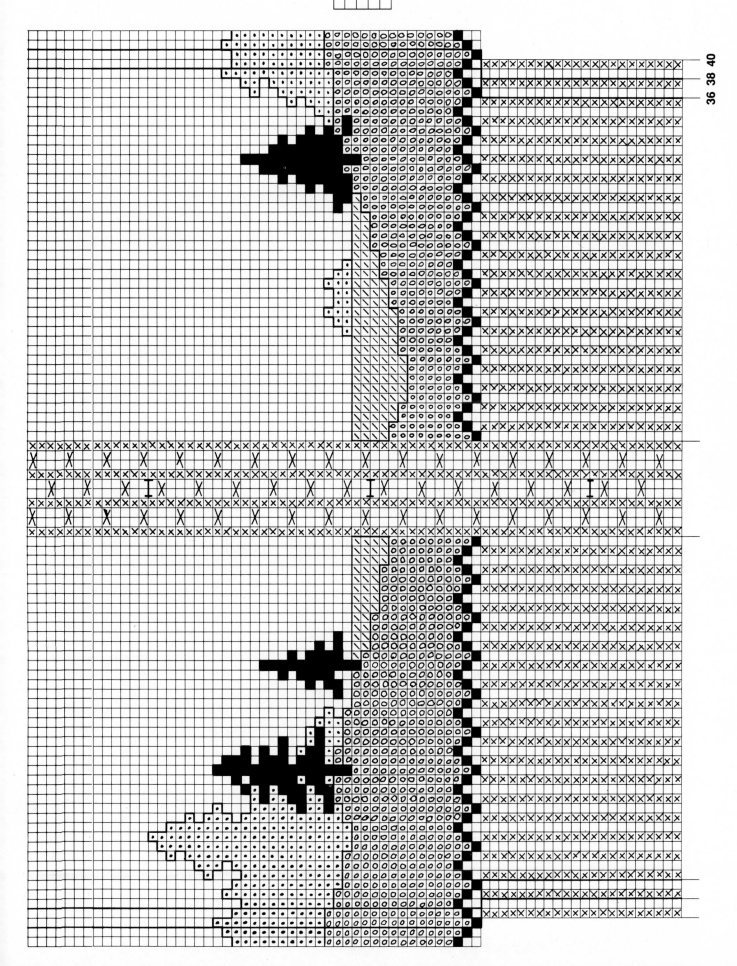

36 38 40

Island Spruce Cardigan

ISLAND SPRUCE CARDIGAN

Most mornings, I savor my first cup of coffee and watch the sky brighten through two enormous, elderly spruce trees....

Sizes: 36 (38, 40)
Finished Sizes: 38 (40, 42)"
Length to underarm: approx 15"
Needles:
    Size 5 and 8 or size needed to obtain stitch gauge of 41/2 sts = 1" using larger needle over stockinette stitch
Materials:
    4 4 oz skeins Natural (MC) worsted weight yarn (800 yds)
    2 4 oz skeins Charcoal Gray worsted weight yarn (400 yds)
    1 4 oz skein Medium Green worsted weight yarn (200 yds)
    1 4 oz skein Spice worsted weight yarn (200 yds)
    75 yds Dark Green worsted weight yarn
    30 yds Medium Blue
    6 Pewter buttons
    Bobbins

☐ NOTES

Length from lower edge to underarm is approx 15" after blocking. Any adjustment in body length should be worked where indicated on chart.
The "tree trunk" is worked in Charcoal Gray, though for simplification it is not indicated on the chart.

☐ PATTERN STITCHES

Mock Cable Twist — knit 2 tog and reknit first st before slipping to other needle. This is always done on right side of work.

☐ BACK

With smaller needles and Charcoal Gray, cast on 82 (86, 90) sts. Turn, wrong side facing, work first 36 (38, 40) sts in K1, P1 ribbing; work center 10 sts as follows: (K1, P2) 3 times, K1; and remaining 36 (38, 40) sts in P1, K1 ribbing. ***Start chart*** and work for 22 rows. Inc 3 sts evenly spaced on each side of tree — 88 (92, 96) sts. Change to larger needles. *Armhole shaping:* At beg of next 2 rows, bind off 5 sts. Dec 1 st at each end of needle every other row 5 times. Work to top of chart, ending with wrong side row. Place all sts on a large holder, leaving MC attached.

ISLAND SPRUCE CARDIGAN

LEFT FRONT

With smaller needles and Charcoal Gray, cast on 46 (48, 50) sts. Turn, wrong side facing, work first 10 sts (K1, P2) 3 times, K1, then work last 36 (38, 40) sts in K1, P1 ribbing. On last row of ribbing, slip 10 sts of "tree trunk" to small holder and inc 3 sts evenly spaced across row. Change to larger needles. Work as for Back to neck opening. *Shape neck:* place 5 sts on holder at neck edge, dec 1 st every other row at neck edge 4 times.

When chart is completed, end with a right-side row and place sts on holder. With smaller needles and Charcoal Gray, work 10 sts of buttonband as shown on chart. Band should be about 1" shorter than sweater front. Press both and stretch band slightly to fit. From back side, slip-stitch band to Front. Arrange buttons on band, reserving 1 button for neckband.

RIGHT FRONT

Work a mirror image of Left Front, remembering to work buttonholes as follows: on wrong-side row after center mock cable twist, work to last 6 sts. Bind off 2 sts, work to end. Next row, cast on 2 sts firmly above bound-off sts.

SHOULDERS

Work across first 20 (22, 24) sts of Back using larger needles; leave rem sts on holder, turn, work back to armhole edge. Place Right Front against Back, right sides tog. Using a third needle, knit 2 shoulder sts tog, 1 from Back and 1 from Front. Knit 2 more sts tog, then bind off 1 st. Continue across row until all sts are bound off. Break yarn, slip through last st.

Leaving center 28 sts on holder, attach MC and work across Back to armhole edge. Place Left Front against Back, right sides tog, and knit shoulders tog. Break yarn, slip through last st.

NECKBAND

Row 1: With smaller needles and Charcoal Gray, right side facing, work 10 buttonband sts, attach Green and K5 sts on holder, pick up and K12 (12, 18) sts up right Front, K28 sts on Back holder, pick up and K13, (13, 19) sts down left Front, K5 sts on holder, drop Green, work 10 sts in Charcoal Gray for buttonband — 83 (83, 95) sts.

Row 2: Work 10 sts in Charcoal Gray for buttonband, attach white, purl to last 10 sts, work 10 sts in Charcoal Gray for buttonband, remembering to work last buttonhole.

Rows 3–7: Continue neck chart, ending with a right-side row. **Chart complete.**

Row 8: Wrong side facing, bind off first 10 sts, with Green, *YO, P2 tog, rep from *, work last 10 sts in Charcoal Gray for buttonband.

Row 9: Bind off first 10 sts. Attach White and work 6 rows stockinette st for hem. Change to larger needles, work 1 more row, then bind off loosely so hem won't pull. Slip stitch hem in place. With right sides tog, sew Back to Fronts at underarm, using backstitch.

SLEEVES

With smaller needles and Charcoal Gray, cast on 42 sts. Work K1, P1 rib for 20 rows, inc 4 sts evenly spaced on last row. Change to larger needles and **start chart**. Inc 1 st each end of needle every 6th row 7 (8, 9) times. When sleeve measures 16 (16½, 17)" or desired length to underarm, *shape Sleeve cap:* At beg of next 2 rows, bind off 5 sts. Dec 1 st each end of needle every other row until 24 sts remain. Bind off 3 sts beg next 4 rows. Bind off remaining 12 sts.

Press sleeves. Right sides tog, sew underarm seam using a backstitch. Turn body of sweater wrong side out. Slip sleeve cap into armhole right sides tog and match underarm and shoulder. Ease sleeve cap to fit. Sew, using backstitch.

Weave in ends.

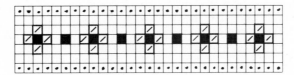

ISLAND SPRUCE CARDIGAN

Neckband

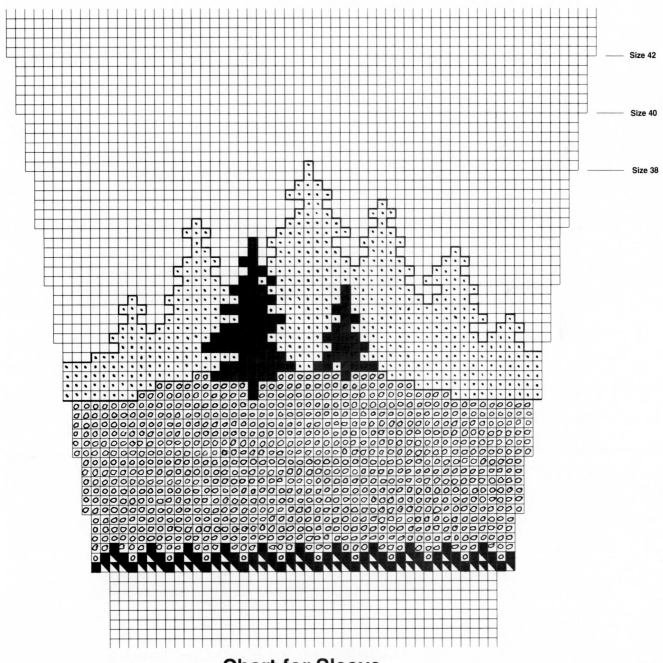

Size 42

Size 40

Size 38

Chart for Sleeve

⊡ = **Medium Green**   ◨ = **Gray**   ◪ = **Blue**   ■ = **Dark Green**   ⊘ = **Spice**

Women's Starry Night Pullover

Men's Starry Night Pullover

WOMEN'S STARRY NIGHT PULLOVER

Sizes: 34 (36, 38, 40)
Finished Sizes: 36 (38, 40, 42)"
Needles:
   Size 5 and 8 or size needed to obtain stitch
   gauge of 41/2 sts = 1" using larger needles
   over stockinette stitch
   Size 5 16" circular needle
Materials:
   5 4 oz skeins Navy (MC) worsted weight
   yarn (1000 yds)
   11/2 4 oz skeins Medium Blue worsted
   weight yarn (300 yds)
   10 yds White fingering yarn

☐ FRONT

With smaller needles and MC, cast on 78
(82, 86, 90) sts. Work in K1, P1 ribbing for
31/4", inc 4 sts evenly spaced on last row of
ribbing. Change to larger needles and work in
stockinette st until piece measures 13 (14,
141/2, 15)" or approximately 1" less than
desired length to underarm. **Begin body
chart.** Work Armhole shaping as follows: bind
off 5 (5, 5, 7) sts at beg of next 2 rows. Dec 1
st each end of needle every other row 4 (6, 6,
6) times. Work straight as per chart until
neck shaping, ending on wrong-side row.
Right side facing, work 23 (23, 25, 25) sts,
place center 18 sts on holder, join new ball of
yarn and work to end of row. Working both
sides at the same time, at each neck edge dec
1 st every other row 4 times. Work to end of
chart binding off shoulders as per chart.

Charts: see pages 78 and 79.

☐ BACK

Work as for Front except neck shaping. Work
to end of chart and bind off shoulder sts as
per chart. Place 26 center Back sts on holder.
Press both Front and Back pieces and
embroider "stars." Sew Front and Back
shoulders together.

☐ NECK

With smaller circular needle and Medium
Blue, pick up and K74 sts around neck
including sts on holders. Work 11/4" in
stockinette st. *Next Row:* *K2 tog, YO*,
repeat between *s to end of row. Continue in
stockinette st for 11/4". *Last row:* using larger
needle, bind off very loosely. Press hem to
inside and hem loosely. Make sure sweater
will go over head easily.

☐ SLEEVES

With smaller needles and MC, cast on 38
(38, 40, 42) sts. Work ribbing same as for
Front for 31/4", inc 4 sts evenly spaced on last
row of ribbing. Change to larger needles and
work in stockinette st, inc 1 st each end of
needle every 8th row 8 times until piece
measures 15 (151/2, 151/2, 16)" or
approximately 1" less than desired length to
underarm. **Begin sleeve chart.** *Sleeve cap:*
bind off 5 (5, 5, 7) sts at beg of next 2 rows.
Dec 1 st each end of needle every other row
until 28 sts remain. Dec 1 st each end of
needle *every* row until 14 sts remain. Bind off
remaining sts. Press sleeves and embroider
"stars."

☐ FINISHING

Set in sleeves, sew remaining seams, weave in
all ends.

Men's Starry Night Pullover

Sizes: 38 (40, 42)
Finished Sizes: 40 (42, 44)"
Needles:
 Size 5 and 8 or size needed to obtain stitch gauge of 41/2 sts = 1" using larger needles over stockinette stitch
 Size 5 16" circular needle
Materials:
 7 4 oz skeins Navy (MC) worsted weight yarn (1400 yds)
 11/2 4 oz skeins Medium Blue worsted weight yarn (300 yds)
 10 yds White fingering yarn

☐ FRONT

With smaller needles and MC, cast on 92 (96, 100) sts. Work in K1, P1 ribbing for 31/2". Change to larger needles and work in stockinette st until piece measures 151/2 (16, 161/2)" or approximately 1" less than desired length to underarm. **Begin body chart.** *Work Armhole shaping* as follows: Bind off 5 (4, 6) sts at beg of next 2 rows. Dec 1 st each end of needle every other row 5 (7, 6) times. Work straight as per chart until neck shaping, ending on wrong-side row. Right side facing, work 26 (28, 28) sts, place center 20 sts on holder, join new ball of yarn and work to end of row. Working both sides at the same time, at each neck edge dec 1 st every other row 4 times. Work to end of chart binding off shoulders as per chart.

☐ BACK

Work as for Front except neck shaping. Work to end of chart binding off shoulders as per chart. Place 28 center Back sts on holder. Press both Front and Back pieces and embroider "stars." Sew Front and Back shoulders together.

☐ NECK

With smaller circular needle and Medium Blue, pick up and K84 sts around neck including sts on holders. Work 11/4" in stockinette st. *Next Row:* *K2 tog, YO* repeat between *s to end of row. Continue in stockinette st for 11/4". *Last row:* using larger needle, bind off very loosely. Press hem to inside and hem loosely. Make sure sweater will go over head easily.

☐ SLEEVES

With smaller needles and MC, cast on 50 (52, 54) sts. Work ribbing same as for Front for 31/2", inc 4 sts evenly spaced on last row of ribbing. Change to larger needles and work in stockinette st, inc 1 st each end of needle every 8th row 8 (7, 8) times until piece measures 17 (18, 19)" or approximately 1" less than desired length to underarm — 70 (70, 74) sts. **Begin sleeve chart.** *Sleeve cap:* bind off 5 (4, 6) sts at beg of next 2 rows. Dec 1 st each end of needle every other row 11 (12, 12) times. Bind off 3 sts beg next 6 rows. Bind off rem sts. Press sleeves and embroider "stars."

☐ FINISHING

Set in sleeves, sew remaining seams, weave in all ends.

Charts: see pages 80 and 81.

SMALL-TOWN GOVERNMENT

The government on an island is never far removed from the people. You or your friends are the elected officials. Meetings are never very far away, and everything major that happens is talked about by nearly everybody, including the kids in school.

When it comes to being an elected or appointed "official," eventually anyone who wants to be involved gets a chance. In fact, the problem is often not how to participate, but how not to. Like most small towns, we have to fill many of the same positions that a larger town does, but from a much smaller pool. Since not everyone even wants to take a turn at these roles, the field narrows even more. In 1989 there were fifty-two elected officials and forty-three appointed posts in our town. This adds up to ninety-five, out of a population of four hundred to pick from—

about eighty-five of them children. That's a big chunk of the population. Of course, there is plenty of overlap, with people serving in more than one capacity, but ninety-five town positions is clearly a lot of jobs for a small town to fill.

Some of the jobs are more demanding than others: school board, planning board, and selectman's position come to mind. These committees tend to address controversial matters and involve weekly or monthly meetings. Other committees are less taxing. Such groups as the local park commission and the alewives committee rarely get into much trouble. Of course, last year we had a huge storm that blew down hundreds of trees at the park, and that gave the park committee something to chew over. They even called a special meeting to appropriate the funds for tree removal.

The alewives committee has never had to raise much more than their annual two hundred dollars, which is used to send a truck to pick up alewives. Alewives are small fish used for lobster-fishing bait. The fish make an annual migration into fresh water to spawn. They are generally caught in the rivers on the mainland during their migration. When they arrive on the island, via truck, these alewives are transplanted to the "fresh pond," which is connected by a stream to the ocean and which used to have a substantial alewife population. Unfortunately, we have never been able to get the fish population large enough here for the fishermen to harvest the alewives for bait. But I find it comforting to know that a branch of our government is out there trying every year.

Of course, one can't just move to town and run for election. Newcomers rarely even vie for a position. When new residents do think they have been around long enough, they usually start out running for something tame, such as medical services—they help out at blood-pressure clinics and with flu shots. They may try for the recreation council, which plans such events as dances and swimming lessons. These activities are usually not too controversial, unless there is a "tight-spending" feeling in the community.

When it comes to deciding who is elected to what, the mood of the community seems to change from year to year. Often the mood determines who will get elected. One year it may be natives who have the edge, and the next year it may be transplants. Some years it seems like older, retired summer people can get elected to anything, even if they just moved to the island the week before. Of course, eager candidates occasionally pack the meeting with family members or supporters, and such tactics can sway the vote, even if it goes against the tide of political feeling.

All this electing takes place at the town meeting, which is the political heart of the community. Town meeting takes place on the first Monday in March, right at the time of year when the long, hard winter has just about got the best of everyone. We all meet at nine in the morning at the "community building"—the gym, the only building large enough to hold us all. Like the elections, a town meeting has a personality of its own that varies from year to year. Some town meetings mean hours of hostile confrontations; others are short, with low attendance and everyone home by lunchtime. At town meeting the community decides where every penny of the municipal budget will be spent that year, and the elections decide who will spend those pennies for us.

Because nominations are taken from the floor, we often don't know who the candidates will be until seconds before we vote. People can decide at the last minute to run for office, and voting can take forever if there are several candidates for a job. For each position, the chosen candidate's name is written on a small piece of white paper, which the voter carries to the ballot box.

When everyone is done, a group of three sitting at a card table on stage count the votes. If there is a majority, voting is complete and the new officeholder is sworn in on the spot by the town clerk, who also sits on the stage (and has held this office for over thirty years). Those elected begin their jobs immediately—and may attend their first meeting that night.

In a town this size, *everyone* knows *everyone*, and our lives are woven together in a tight web. When it's time to debate the issues, either for or against, you may be arguing against your co-workers, your friends, or the person who is installing the new sink in your kitchen. People often reveal opinions or strong feelings that you never knew they had. And you may occasionally find yourself arguing with more passion than you realized you felt. The major surprise in town meeting is that we all recover from whatever lines are drawn and whatever insults are flung. Like siblings who are in the relationship for the long haul, we can often survive more heated disagreements than can those who are passing acquaintances. Although grudges do exist here, and some families don't talk to each other for years, we all have a tie, and it takes more than a few harsh words to break it.

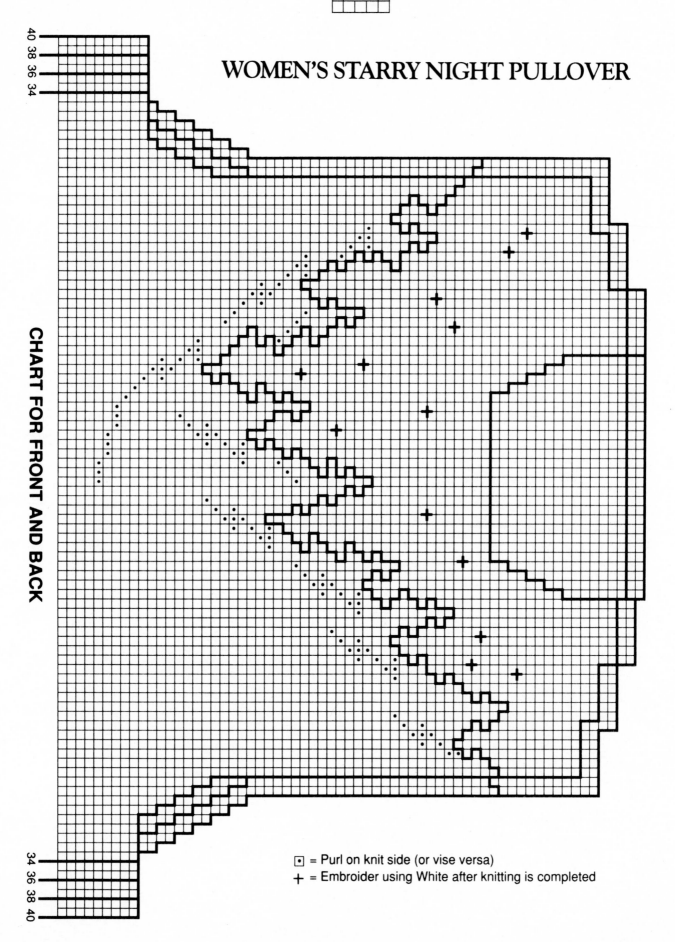

WOMEN'S STARRY NIGHT PULLOVER

CHART FOR FRONT AND BACK

☐• = Purl on knit side (or vise versa)
+ = Embroider using White after knitting is completed

WOMEN'S STARRY NIGHT PULLOVER

SLEEVE CAP

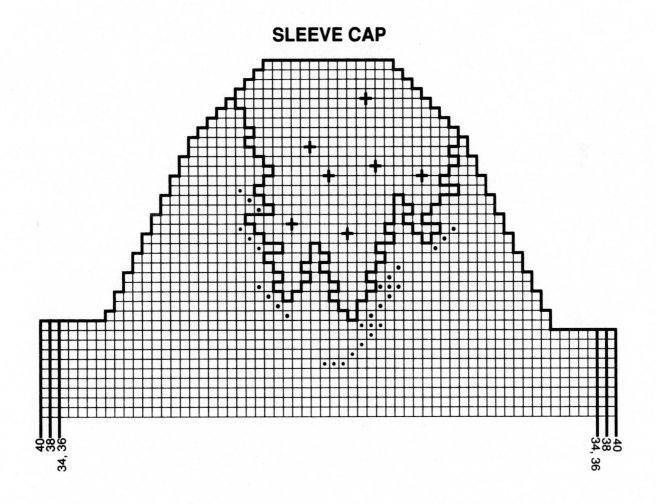

40
38
34, 36

40
38
34, 36

MEN'S STARRY NIGHT PULLOVER

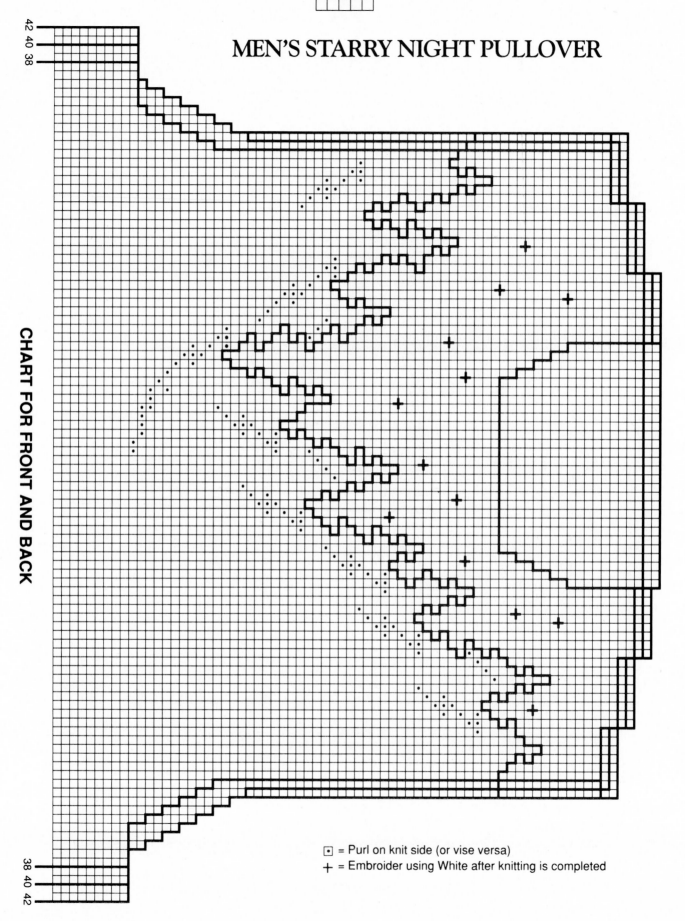

CHART FOR FRONT AND BACK

42 40 38

38 40 42

⊡ = Purl on knit side (or vise versa)
✛ = Embroider using White after knitting is completed

MEN'S STARRY NIGHT PULLOVER

SLEEVE CAP

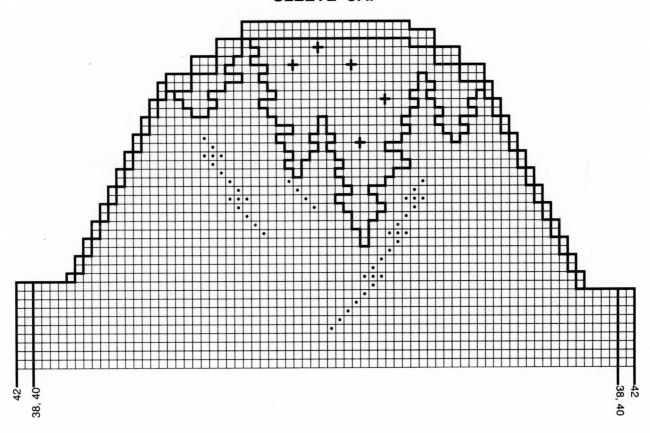

Tropical Fish Pullover

Tropical Fish
Pullover

Sizes: 36 (38, 40)
Finished Sizes: 38 (40, 42)"
Needles:
    Size 5 and 8 or size needed to obtain stitch
    gauge of 41/2 sts = 1" using larger needles
    over stockinette stitch
    Size E Crochet hook
    Bobbins
Materials:
    7 31/2 oz skeins Sky Blue (MC)
    50%Cotton/50% Wool (1200 yds)
    60 yds Aqua
    50 yds Purple
    20 yds Bright Pink
    20 yds Light Yellow
    10 yds Dark Yellow
    10 yds Dark Blue

☐ NOTES
Use bobbins or short strands of color and
separate balls of Main Color (MC) between
fish rather than carry colors very far.

☐ PATTERN STITCHES
Bubbles — The bubbles are always done in a
Knit stitch. K in front, in back, and in front
of same stitch; turn, P3; turn, K3 together.

☐ FRONT
With smaller needles and MC, cast on 77
(82, 87) sts. *Rows 1 and 3:* K1, *P1, K2, P1,
K1, rep from *, end K1. *Row 2 and all even-
numbered rows:* Knit the knits and purl the
purls. *Row 5 and every 6th row thereafter:* K1,
*P1, K2 tog then reknit first K st to form
mock cable, P1, K1, rep from *, end K1.
Continue until ribbing measures 21/2",
increasing 7 (8, 9) sts evenly spaced across
last row of ribbing. Change to larger needles
and work 4 rows stockinette st. **Work Chart
A** inc 2 (0, 0) sts on last row, 86 (90, 96) sts.
Work 0 (2, 4) rows stockinette st. **Work
Main Chart**. Work until piece measures
151/2 (151/2, 16)" or desired length to
underarm. *Armhole shaping:* At beg of next 2
rows, bind off 6 sts. Dec 1 st at each end of

needle every other row 7 times – 60 (64, 68)
sts. Work until armhole measures 6 (6, 61/2)".
Work 19 (21, 23) sts, bind off center 22 sts
loosely, work remaining 19 (21, 23) sts.
Working both sides at the same time (join
another ball of yarn), dec 1 st at neck edge
every row 3 times. Place 16 (18, 20) shoulder
sts on holders.

☐ BACK
Work same as Front through **Chart A**. Parts
of Main Chart can be used, or just straight
knitting as desired. (You may, for example,
wish to do one little fish with bubbles
halfway up Back.) Work armholes same as
Front until they measure 7 (7, 71/2)". Work
18 (20, 22) sts, bind off center 24 sts loosely,
work remaining 18 (20, 22) sts. Working
both sides at the same time (join another ball
of yarn), dec 1 st at neck edge every row
twice. Place 16 (18, 20) shoulder sts on
holders.

☐ SLEEVES
With smaller needles, cast on 42 sts working
ribbing same as Front for 21/2", inc 6 (8, 10)
sts evenly across last row of ribbing. Change
to larger needles and work 4 rows stockinette
st. **Work Chart A** and *at the same time*, inc
1 st each end of needle every 6th row 5 (5, 6)
times. (Here again, an occasional little fish
with bubbles is effective.) Work until sleeve
measures 16 (161/2, 17)" or desired length to
underarm.
Sleeve cap: At beg of next 2 rows, bind off 6
sts. Dec 1 st each end of needle every other
row until 20 sts remain. Dec 1 st each end
every row 4 times. Bind off remaining sts.

☐ FINISHING
Place shoulder sts of Front and Back right-
sides together. Using a third needle, knit the
shoulders together and bind off the sts. To
finish neck, work 1 row single crochet using a
contrasting color. Set in sleeves, sew
remaining seams and weave in all ends.

TROPICAL FISH PULLOVER

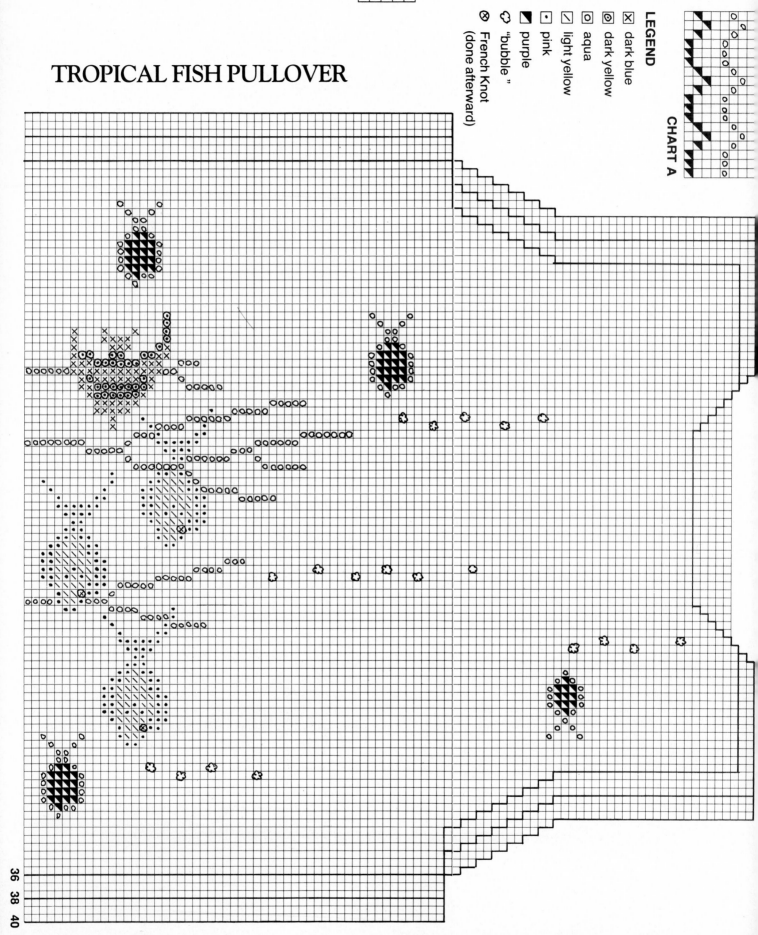

LEGEND

- ☒ dark blue
- ⊘ dark yellow
- ⊡ aqua
- ⊿ light yellow
- ⊡ pink
- ◼ purple
- ♧ "bubble"
- ⊗ French Knot (done afterward)

CHART A

Northern Lights

It is a clear night in the late winter and an excited friend calls us: there is a chance to observe the spectacular beauty of the northern lights. We rush outside to see the phenomenal display—red in the eastern and western sky, green to the south. A white dome caps the sky, with spokes of light cascading out in every direction. After staring with that heart-pounding feeling that comes with seeing something that can't be explained, we all rush in to call other friends, just to make sure no one misses this phenomenon. My daughter calls everyone she can think of, plus a few more people I have suggested. As she hangs up the phone, three people call us. The next morning on the ferry people ask each other if they witnessed the display.

The northern lights, the aurora borealis, can be observed in many places. They are produced by highly charged particles exciting the gases of the upper atmosphere and making them glow, filling the sky with shooting lights and colors. In a northern state such as ours, the northern lights can be seen as often as twenty-five times a year. They represent one of the amazing benefits of living in a place where the sky is clear.

Although watching the northern lights in your front yard is a very personal experience, in our town we often share such events. We call each other to announce it, discuss it the next day, catalog each other's responses, and reconsider our own. The way we share the experience is an example of all that we share throughout the year—information, time, and our feelings.

In a small town we share a lot of feelings as a community. A death saddens everyone and must be discussed for days as everyone comes to terms with the loss. Basketball games, the annual science fair, and Christmas events are often attended by more than just the parents involved, as everyone shares in the joys of our children's successes.

The sound of the fire whistle brings us all to life like nothing else. There is no way of knowing, upon first hearing the whistle, where the fire may be; but we can be sure that it is burning at a business or home belonging to someone we know. Within minutes nearly every vehicle in the village is headed in the direction of the fire station. The first volunteers will jump into the trucks, and once they are gone, a message on the blackboard will state the location of the fire. Many observers will follow, and those who hear the whistle and stay at home or work will often be on the phone anxiously trying to determine what is going on. Luckily, most of the alarms announce a minor or manageable problem, such as a chimney fire or a grass fire that has gone out of control. Until this is confirmed, however, everyone worries.

In a small town, volunteering is the rule. Besides all the civic and governmental offices to be filled, people volunteer on their own to do various jobs around the community. Every April there is a crew that cleans the roadsides with the kids, and every Christmas two brothers put a tree up in the town square. People serve on the ambulance crew and help the kids produce plays and raise money for trips. The list is endless and includes unorganized activities as well. When someone is sick, friends often bring over food or just help out. People take care of each other's kids, offer to run errands on the mainland, and offer anyone on foot a ride.

Because of the geographic and cultural boundaries of our island, we understand our dependence on each other. But no town or society could ever afford to "pay" for all the things that must be done, and the survival of any community depends on its residents' willingness to cooperate and share.

HALLOWEEN

Halloween is one of my favorite holidays on the island. It is a night of freedom and abundance for children—the streets belong to them, and wandering through the darkness is no longer scary but leads to great rewards. Many wonderful homemade creations are displayed on the streets, and whole crowds of "punk" girls or vampires may pass by, each with its own variation on the theme.

Adults share in Halloween night, too. They treat children with homemade snacks or load the treat bags down with great quantities of a favorite snack from their childhood. There is no suspicion when the children come home and open their bags—they know who made the candies, know they are safe. Some of the door-tenders dress up as witches and ghosts and ghouls, daring the children to take the candy for their bags.

Over the years many people have created haunted houses for all to enter, but one family has continued the tradition for many years. The oldest brother (of eleven children) has a large house in the center of town, and he, along with his brothers and others, conspires to scare out of their wits all who enter (while still being friendly to the very small). When my children were little, I looked forward to taking them out so that I would have a reason to step inside this legendary house. The first years were spent frustrated at the bottom step where the ghouls would linger, attempting to draw in unsuspecting souls. A very young child would leave at this point, preferring to wait until next year. Finally I raised a child or two old enough to go in and was able to take a first-hand look at what was inside.

The first year was the best, and I am sure it was because I was feeling a little terror myself. We walked up the long stairs to the house, and once inside we were instructed to enter the small room off the entryway. Two or three blood-stained individuals holding axes and other tools of destruction invited us in and asked if we would like some candy. We nodded our heads, and one of the scary guys lifted the cover off a huge platter on the table. On the platter next to the giant candy bars was a disgusting bloody head that spoke with a friendly voice. We grabbed a candy bar, forgot our thank-you's, and escaped.

Regrouped at the bottom of the hill in front of the house, we were confident that there was probably a hole in the table and a body that connected to the head. Calm once again settled over us. We had faced our demons, received our reward, and run before it was too late—another Halloween had served us well.

ABOUT
OUR MODELS

Writing about the models is one of my favorite tasks in preparing these books. It gives me an opportunity to appreciate again the many people who are willing to let us put them through the torture of being photographed. Aside from being uncertain about how the photographs will turn out, the models all willingly go through the trial of the photographing day itself.

Of course, there is an element of fun in these days when we load up cars and trucks with sweaters, turtlenecks, people, and occasionally props (remember the pet chickens of earlier books?). Depending on the weather, we drive around the island looking for the right light and inspiration. I always start the car in low gear, thinking that we should just travel to one of our tried and true spots, and Peter, our faithful photographer, battles with me, knowing that we can come up with something new and different. The models wait patiently as we travel to different locations, searching for the right setting for each sweater.

Some of these days are ideal—not too sunny (reduces squinting and shadows), with a light breeze to keep the wool sweaters from melting everyone. Of course it doesn't always work out that way.

This year we had a whole day of pouring rain. We spent the day searching for covered porches and open barns—places with sufficient natural light so that we wouldn't have to deal with artificial lights. Although a hot day can be unbearable in a wool sweater, all our models would agree that the cold is worse. When we shoot outside on a cold day, the models have to concentrate very hard to keep from shivering during the exposure. We all take turns telling them to think about hot summer days or the beaches of Hawaii, in hopes that they can somehow will their noses and hands not to turn red for the photos.

On page 14 you can find Nancy, a loyal model since the beginning. Nancy's mother, Marion, was the first North Island Design employee, and although Marion has since retired, Nancy keeps the family connection alive. Nancy has four children under ten, is active in community affairs, runs a day care center, and teaches aerobics. She owns a building that houses both professions, which is called "Nancy's Body Shop and Parts Place."

One of Nancy's children, Quincy, appears on page 15. Quincy is a great seven-year-old, much loved by her friends and teachers. On the rainy day she and her mother posed with this flock of sheep, Quincy was amazing to photograph—she stood very still, concentrated on what she was doing, and never seemed to blink. She was a quiet kid at age five, but today, although it is clear she is a deep thinker, she is a great conversationalist with an entertaining sense of humor and a wonderful imagination.

Christie is on our cover wearing everyone's favorite sweater in a field of lupines. That was one of those winning photos which come as a last-minute inspiration. We were just wrapping up a long day and the light was fading fast when we drove by a field of lupines in full bloom. With the light disappearing and the mosquitos descending on Christie, Peter snapped away but took as few photographs as possible because we were all eager to be done. We ended up with one of our best photos of the most popular sweater of all time, and we were even able to find a slide without a bug on Christie's face.

Jessie, Christie's stepdaughter (page 28), never takes a bad photo, and we are always glad when she is in town on photo-shooting day. Jessie is in college and is only here in the summers, when she works at the family inn, helps a gardener, and teaches swimming lessons—very busy. Amanda, another stepdaughter with a great smile (page 29), has also been one of our good-natured standbys whenever she is in town. She, too, is a college student who helps to manage the inn for the summer and is spending fall at sea.

Eliza (page 40) is a lively, friendly model with a wonderful smile. She is always a joy to have around when she and her family visit in the summer, whether we are photographing or not. Eliza is in her last year of college and thinking seriously of becoming a teacher; she would be a great addition to the profession. With a father who is a primatologist, this wonderfully close family had the good fortune of traveling together during the summers when he was doing work with baboons and other wildlife in such exotic locations as Kenya and Sierra Leone.

Hannah and Asa, two of my children, appear in the photo on page 64. Hannah is fourteen and Asa nine. Of course, hand in hand isn't the pose they strike all the time, being siblings with all the rivalry and fighting that entails. However, I do envy them growing up together in a rural community where, with the absence of so many distractions, siblings seem to spend more time together and grow up as close friends. Being a part of our small school (about sixty-five students kindergarten through twelfth grade) means that they are together each day, in different wings of the same building. They may visit each other's classrooms and occasionally participate in the same school events, or an older child like Hannah may take a turn helping with the lower grades and work with Asa's class. All these are very special connections that are often lost in our busy and modern world.

One other family member, myself, appears on page 57. This photo is from the archives as I now actually prefer to be on the other side of the camera, coaching the models to smile and negotiating with Peter about what to shoot next.

Jon, in the Men's Starry Night, is pictured on page 73. Jon works with my husband as a boatbuilder and is also active in many community activities such as editing our local newspaper and serving on the five-person board of selectmen, which meets weekly to discuss matters affecting our town. Jon moved here eighteen years ago to build boats, and fish for lobsters and scallops, and to seine for herring, which he did for many years.

I can't let a discussion of this photo of Jon pass without mentioning the time we took a poster of it to a big trade show where thousands of buyers came to look at our designs. The sweater sold very well, and the poster attracted a lot of attention. Our favorite response was from one woman who stopped to look and asked who he was. I said "my neighbor," to which she replied, "Don't move!"

David, who is pictured with Christie on page 76, is shown wearing one of his many hats—sorting the mail for rural delivery. A fisherman for many years, David has now moved his career onshore, where he delivers the mail, works as a caretaker, occasionally helps out at the family burger shop/fish market that his wife runs, and generally plays an important role in our community. With a deep, booming voice, David is always called on when a banquet needs a special kind of performer. David has long been committed to the kids and school, serving for years on the school board and as a basketball coach, not to mention being the owner of the best Halloween haunted house in town.

Franklin, another fixture of our community, is a member of the family that runs the store at the head of the ferry landing, which has been operating in this location since the 1920s. Franklin puts in long hours during the busy summer season and also is in the store five days a week all winter. This is one of those "general stores" where your meat is cut to order, the kids swamp the candy counter all summer and after school, and regulars gather for coffee on winter mornings and watch the ferry pull out.

DESIGN YOUR OWN

Again in this book we decided to include two blank grids to give you the opportunity to do some designing of your own. Our favorite pullover, the versatile cable design, has a wonderful yoke and sleeve that lends itself to almost any pattern you can create. Using the two grids that follow and the compatible patterns, we encourage you to design your own sweater.

First we suggest, be brave and don't think twice about your ability to do this. We all have some designs tucked away in us somewhere and this is your chance to bring them out. If you can't think of anything, look in a favorite cross stitch pattern book—those patterns are very adaptable and they are already charted for you.

Begin by taking these pages of blank grids to a photocopier and making several copies. This will give you lots of opportunities to try different ideas and perfect them. As you work on them—think about your hobbies or a favorite animal. Are you a wildflower or exotic bird fancier? Does your grandchild have a special stuffed animal or your son or daughter a favorite sport?

Once you have chosen your design, here are a few suggestions about working with motif-type designs that we have learned over the years:
• Keep the design in from the edges—you don't want to lose a critical element to the curve in a person's body.
• The major theme should be off center for the best look.
• Odd numbers of objects are usually better.
• When you are using several different colors of yarn, leave the texture stitches to a minimum, and when using lots of texture, keep the number of colors to a minimum.
• Give designing a try—remember you can always rip it out and replace it with one of the designs we have provided.

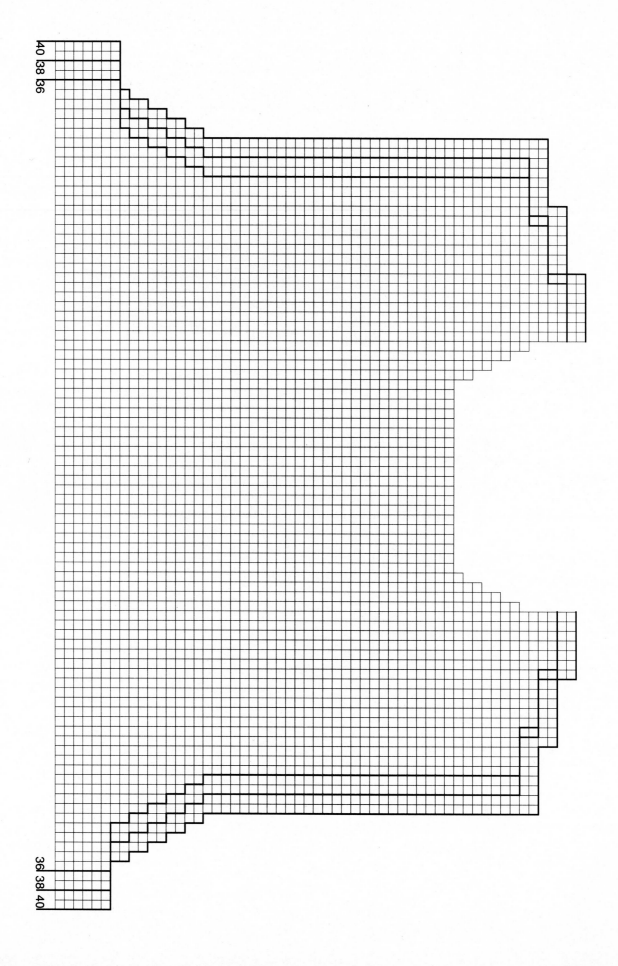

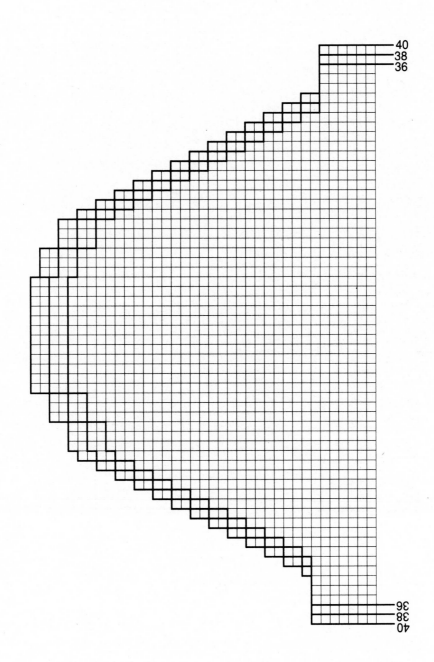

40
38
36

36
38
40

SOURCES OF SUPPLY

If you do not have a good local source for the materials to make the sweaters in this book, they are all available through us. We sell kits, skeined yarns, and yarn packs (all of the yarns needed to create one of these designs, packaged together in just the right quantities). We also produce a catalog that includes many knitting kits not featured in this book, as well as accessories such as buttons and wooden knitting needles. You can call us toll free to place an order, to ask a knitting question, or just to check on our weather. Add your name to our mailing list to receive our newsletter—we'll keep you updated on our new designs and stories of island life.

North Island Designs
Main Street
North Haven, ME 04853
1-800-548-5648
207-867-4788 (Maine and Canada)

For those of you who would like more information about loons and what you can do to help, two organizations to contact are:

North American Loon Fund
RR #4 Box 240C
High Street
Meredith, NH 03253-9416
603-279-6163

Loon Project
Maine Audubon Society
118 US Route One
Falmouth, ME 04105
207-781-2330

If you would like to receive more information about the islands of Maine, their history and future, you can contact:

The Island Institute
60 Ocean Street
Rockland, ME 04841
207-594-9209

LOON (cont.)

Continued from page 45

anything that passed by, the migrating loons suffered further setbacks. They were also considered great sport on the lakes because marksmen would never know where they were going to reappear after they dived. In all these cases, the birds were never shot for food, only for entertainment.

The Migratory Bird Treaty Act of 1918 slowed these losses, but human beings continue to threaten the loon. Unfortunately, the problems the loon faces today are more complex and difficult to solve. Over-development on northern lakes has significantly decreased the available nesting spots, as houses and docks take up space that was once wild. When loons do nest on inhabited lakes, they occasionally abandon their nests when disturbed by curious onlookers or when their nests are washed away by the wakes from boats or water-skiers. Other threats such as pollution and oil spills in their winter nesting grounds have taken a toll.

Perhaps the biggest problem today is acid rain in the northern lakes. These acids are produced in the atmosphere when emissions from power plants, factories, and automobiles combine with the rain. When this rain falls to the earth, it releases metals in the soil, which are eventually washed into the streams and lakes. Many of these metals, such as mercury and aluminum, are toxic to the insects and fish in the lake and, through the food chain, to the loons. Birds such as the loons suffer directly from mercury poisoning and indirectly from the reduction in their food supply.

The plight of the loon—resulting from a combination of pollution from many sources, our changing use of the "wilderness," and the loon's inability to evolve fast enough in response to the changes imposed on it in the last one hundred years—reminds us that there are no easy answers to our environmental problems. In today's world, every decision we make must take into consideration the interconnectedness of all life on earth, or else such magnificent creatures as the loons will soon be seen only on sweaters.

Several conservation organizations are actively educating people about loons, organizing counts and creating artificial habitats on lakes where nesting grounds have been threatened or do not exist. Contact organizations in your area or the addresses listed in the sources section to find out more about what you can do to help this wonderful bird.